IGNORE IT!

IGNORE IT!

How Selectively Looking
the Other Way Can Decrease
Behavioral Problems and
Increase Parenting
Satisfaction

CATHERINE PEARLMAN, PhD, LCSW

A TarcherPerigee Book

tarcherperigee

An imprint of Penguin Random House LLC
375 Hudson Street
New York, New York 10014

Most TarcherPerigee books are available at special quantity discounts for
bulk purchase for sales promotions, premiums, fund-raising, and educational
needs. Special books or book excerpts also can be created to fit specific needs.
For details, write: SpecialMarkets@penguinrandomhouse.com.

ISBN 9780143130338

Printed in the United States of America
3   5   7   9   10   8   6   4   2

Book design by Katy Riegel

To Jeff, for all that's still TK.

To Casey and Emmett,

for the inspiration

and letting me practice on them.

And to Norma, you know which one.

Author's Note

In order to de-identify any clients, all of the names of parents and their children have been changed. Some clients who had similar issues or similarly aged children have been combined into one family or scenario. This was done to provide more complete details to client situations and to ensure confidentiality and anonymity. All of these scenarios have occurred in many families over the course of my work. The work I describe with families in this book and the response to Ignore it! are relayed to the best of my recollection.

Contents

Appendixes

If there is anything that we wish to change in the child, we should first examine it and see whether it is not something that could better be changed in ourselves.

—Carl Jung

PART I

Introduction

WHILE STANDING BY your side at the supermarket checkout line, your child begins to whine for a pack of gum.

"Mooooommmmmmmm!" she says in her most irksome tone.

"Not today," you reply.

"Pleeeaaaaassse, Mommy," she says. "Pleeeeaaaassssee . . ."

"No," you say softly, hoping that what you know is going to happen somehow won't.

"Pleaaase, Mommy. It's just gum."

Again, you say, "Not today"—but with more force.

Seeing that you are distracted and getting frustrated, your child—crafty as ever—kicks it into high gear with an extra-annoying, bloodcurdling, screechy whine. Finally, at wits' end, you either:

A. Buy the gum just to make your little darling keep
   quiet.

B. Stop what you are doing to devote three minutes of time to lecture and admonish your child—then immediately feel deflated and angry.

Either way, you lose.

AS A FAMILY COACH, I conduct parenting groups and seminars. I do in-home and phone consultations. I meet with PTAs, religious organizations, and teachers. Strangers in malls and gas stations sometimes ask me my advice after learning of my profession. Inevitably, I am hit with a variation of the very same question. *Why won't my kid behave?*

Or, to be a bit more specific, parents ask:

"Why does my son refuse to sit still at the table?"
"My daughter makes the most annoying noises for no reason. No matter how nicely I ask her to stop or even if I get mad, she still does it. What can I do to make her stop it?"
"When I try to give my son a time-out, he runs around the room. How can I get him to sit for the time-out?"
"One of my sons will do anything to get my attention. He hums, taps his pencil, and nudges his brothers. All day long. What can I do to get him to stop it?"

I've heard them all, and the pattern is as predictable as the morning sun. The child does something undesirable or annoying and the parent tries everything—from begging to screaming to punishing—to curb the behavior. And, unsurprisingly, nothing works.

Kids are not out to get us (although it really may feel that way sometimes). They are kids. The nature of their job is to explore, learn, and develop. The nature of the parenting job is to teach, guide, love, and nurture.

Most parents feel that in order to change behavior, they have to *do* something. But often what they are doing is only encouraging the behavior. That's right. What they are doing is actually making the behavior worse.

In my work as a family coach, I often see parents overdisciplining behaviors that they should ignore and underdisciplining behaviors that they should address. Parents are constantly nagging and trying to get kids to stop doing attention-seeking behaviors. That constant battle of wills is leaving parents exhausted and out of tools. To help parents discipline more effectively, I started to preach *selective ignoring*, a process of strategically overlooking annoying or dysfunctional behavior. Based on well-respected behavior modification research, the idea is to use ignoring deliberately. The concept is usually met with the same initial reaction from parents: "There's no way this will work." Then they try it and the magic begins. They report a decrease in annoying behavior, higher overall parenting satisfaction, and improved parent-child relationships.

I decided to write this book because I saw so many parents struggling with the same issues. And, regrettably, their actions were only making matters worse. In this book, I will teach parents how to reliably minimize or even eliminate unwanted behavior and encourage more positive behavior. What's even more fulfilling is that you could also improve your child's self-esteem and increase your parenting satisfaction. That means that you will actually enjoy your time with your kids more. Who wouldn't sign up for that?

Although the concepts in this book are based on extensive research and experience working with families, I think you will find that it is not complicated or intimidating. It is completely doable—simple concepts explained well, with lots of examples for use.

Sometimes, parents are so at the end of their rope that they can't wait to get to the tools in a parenting book. They read a little here and then a little there. The book stays at the bedside but never gets a parent's full attention. This always makes me sad. Parents are seeking some help, and they reach out for it. But they don't allow themselves to fully prepare for making changes in the way they are interacting with their children. Without reading all about a new technique, they do a brief attempt at implementing a new parenting strategy, only to get confused about how it works. Soon the parent feels this new strategy doesn't work and gives up. When this happens, the parent feels demoralized and out of control. What's worse is that the child learns that parents attempt new ways to curb negative behavior only to give up. This teaches children that parents will sometimes try to introduce new "consequences" for poor behavior, but if the kids work hard at it, they can get them to give it up. Sadly, this means the same negative behaviors—or even worse behaviors—will repeat again and again.

For these reasons, I recommend resisting the temptation to skip ahead in this book. Each chapter builds on the previous one to fully explain the concepts to you. I promise it is a quick and easy read. If you bought this book, it is because you really want to improve your home environment. Give yourself the gift of taking your time to absorb it all. It will be worth it.

This book is organized in three parts. In Part I, you will learn about the theoretical basis for Ignore it!. Here I will teach you about the overdisciplining cycle and the basics of ignoring. I will tell you what to ignore and what you cannot ignore.

Part II of the book is the how-to section. You will learn exactly how to begin ignoring, and I will give you loads of scenarios to illustrate the concepts. I'll also help you understand how to ignore in public, what to do if behavior gets worse at first, and how to manage common impediments to success.

Although Part III strays from the narrow focus of Ignore it!, it is a vital section of the book. Getting rid of unwanted behavior with Ignore it! only solves part of the problem. In Part III, you will learn how to encourage more desirable behaviors and provide consequences to any inappropriate behavior that cannot be ignored. I have listed some frequently asked questions with answers and good tips to help you get started. The very last chapter is my pep talk. In all of my sessions, this is often the most essential part of my engagement with parents. Yes, I provide practical parenting tips in these sessions, and that is clearly important. But what many parents really need is a pep talk. They need to know that *they can make this change*. I support parents and reassure them. With that support, they feel confident to get started making modifications, and that's when their lives change. I will do this here for you, too.

For some parents, Ignore it! will be just one of the tools needed to address the issues of their children's behavior. Additional counseling and support from a licensed therapist,

psychologist, or psychiatrist may be warranted. A full evaluation, medication, and other interventions might be in order to
improve serious or problematic behaviors. Ignore it! can be used
in conjunction with most other therapies. However, do seek
outside help as needed.

READY FOR A CHANGE? Let's go do this thing.

CHAPTER 1

Ignore My Kids? Are You Crazy?

WHENEVER I COUNSEL parents to ignore their children, I receive one of two responses. Roughly half look at me with a tilted head and an expression similar to the one my dog, Norma, makes when she isn't sure what I am saying. They say something like, "Um, what do you mean, *ignore* them?" I repeat my thoughts about ignoring all of the annoying or testing behaviors, and the parents start to wonder if I am a bad family coach. Why on earth would they ignore their children? It feels counterintuitive. Bad behavior doesn't just go away if you ignore it.

Well, actually, it does. (I'll show you why in the next two chapters). After learning about Ignore it!, one dad told me he was scared to ignore his son's inappropriate behavior because he worried the child would think he was okay with it. Dad *wasn't* okay with it, and he wanted to be able to express that to his son. With Ignore it!, he still can convey that message—only not with words. His behavior will speak for him.

The other half of the parents are ecstatic to have permission to ignore their kids. They are exhausted from constant parenting. Managing children, careers, house payments and taxes, elderly parents, birthday parties, and school projects has mothers and fathers on the edge of checking out. Learning what one can and should ignore is often life-changing. One dad, relieved that he could at times ignore his only child, wrote me, "Thank you for this method. Now I can procreate again." I'm pretty sure he was serious.

What isn't disputed by these parents is that they are experiencing highly undesirable behavior from their children. Their kids whine. They cry and yell and scream and tantrum. The kids agitate them, often on purpose. And they push all of Mom and Dad's buttons just because they can. Children are exploiting their parents' vulnerabilities in every town, in every county, in every corner of every state. In response, parents spend more time disciplining than ever before. Time-outs and consequences are in perpetual rotation. Everything is a negotiation. But none of this is working. Not only is the unacceptable behavior not disappearing, it often gets worse.

As behavior gets worse parents yell more and punish more. They are angry and frustrated a lot more. Or, worst of all, they give up and give in. As a result, moms and dads enjoy parenting on a day-to-day basis a lot less. Something has to give. Parents usually choose to have children because while they imagined the hard work, they focused on the intense joy. However, they feel deflated when the balance is off so significantly. They experience considerably more frustration than elation.

Where did they go wrong?

Watch Me, Watch Me, Watch Me

What is really at the heart of the two general parent responses to Ignore it! is that, in this age of relentless child observation, adulation, and adoration, ignoring children seems to be anathema to the predominate parenting style. Hyperparenting is an epidemic. I am not pointing fingers at helicopter parents because, quite honestly, we are all helicoptering to some degree. We never ignore our children. Ever. We take a heightened interest in everything they do, from their homework to their after-school activities to getting them into the best college.

Now, I can almost hear some of you saying, "That isn't me." Okay, maybe there are degrees to helicopter parenting. But read a few phrases most parents hear on a daily basis and ask yourself if you belong in the group:

"Mom, watch me do this dive again."
"Mom, did you see the amazing car I made with my LEGOs?"
"Dad, watch this replay of my insane touchdown on the Xbox."
"Pop, watch me climb this tree."

"Watch me, watch me, watch me." Kids aren't satisfied pleasing themselves. They want to impress their parents and everyone around them, and they want to hear feedback on how (OMG!) awesome they are. Just observe any child playing any sport. A kid makes a great play in soccer and immediately looks to the parent for the thumbs-up. Parents dictate self-worth in early childhood. By middle school, self-worth is decreed by an outside influence and measured in likes, shares, and popularity.

Teens vigilantly craft their online images by posting only carefully curated selfies that have been approved by their best friends.

The need for attention is so great that children will go to extreme lengths to attain it. At first, most aim for the spotlight by being delightful. But sometimes that doesn't work. Parents may have other children to divide their attention. Some parents work from home or are sick or even need a minute to make a call or send an e-mail. This divided attention can lead kids to try to snag attention in less desirable ways. Enter: nudging, testing, needling, whining, yelling, and tantruming.

How and when did all of this attention-seeking and testing behavior start?

It began in infancy, and it was learned. Yup, we taught this behavior to our babies. We don't just let kids watch a *Baby Einstein* video while we take a break from parenting for a half hour. No, we insist on sitting with them to teach them or support them or just keep them safe. Babies nowadays have a lot less self-directed play. In past generations, children didn't have to be learning all the time. They just played without purpose. Those days are long gone.

Kids used to be left up to their own devices much more. They explored freely, rode their bikes around town, walked with their friends to the store for gum. When I was a kid, I'd spend long hours in the basement making "art" out of household products and laundry detergent. If I got bored, I'd walk myself over to the Schwartzes' house to play Risk or Atari or hoops in the driveway. When it was time for my piano lesson, I'd ride my bike to the teacher's house a mile away, *all by myself.* It was great. Times have changed.

This idea of constant parental supervision and instruction isn't just self-imposed by parents. It is coming from all areas of society. For example, take a look at the description for a popular toy called Fisher-Price Brilliant Basics Baby's First Blocks (notice the word "brilliant" in the name). The toy is a bucket containing shaped blocks and topped with a sorting grate. The online description of the toy reads, "Your baby will learn new concepts about colors and shapes (circle, star, triangle, and more) as *the two of you* sort the blocks through the shape-sorting lid before stacking up each group to knock them down." This toy is for a six-month-old. Why would a parent need to sort the blocks *with* the baby? Why can't the baby just play on her own? Answer: because society tells parents they need to constantly engage their attention on their children.

Of course, children require attention from their parents. And parents are usually devoted to providing it. But there is a healthy amount of attention that can turn problematic. More attention doesn't necessarily produce better-adjusted and -behaved children. Once children come to expect endless attention, that attention can turn into a drug, and your kid into an addict. And just like the junkie seeking a fix, children continue attention-seeking behaviors despite undesirable consequences such as yelling and punishment.

The Inmates Are Running the Asylum

There is a natural call-and-response system set up to ensure babies thrive. When even day-old babies need something, like milk or to be changed, they cry. Crying alerts parents that the baby requires assistance. As parents respond quickly to the baby's needs, a secure attachment starts to develop. It is very important for a child to forge a trust that his needs will be met reliably. So what's the downside?

Infants quickly learn that to score a parent's attention, crying gets the job done. Long before children can speak or even use American Sign Language, they learn to communicate through crying. Baby wants milk? He cries. Baby sees a strange face or hears a loud noise? He cries. Baby's angry, frustrated, bored, sad, gassy? Well, he might as well cry. For newborns crying is an innate ability that acts like a survival skill. It's the universal language all parents understand.

Parents work hard to stop that crying, and that's a good thing—at first. But at some point, children are able to tolerate more hunger, frustration, and discomfort. When parents intervene without fail to stop all types of crying, children learn to use it for their advantage. Whimpering and whining gets immediate attention from Mom and Dad, as well as a quick resolution. As children age, they learn to perfect their pitch and—Shazam!—crying becomes tantrums. It turns out parents hate tantrums even more than crying, and will do anything, especially if in public, to end the hysteria. And your kid knows it.

Children, particularly young children, control precious little in their lives. Parents control *everything*. This lopsided power dynamic doesn't sit well with those on the losing end. Kids sometimes challenge parents just because they can. For example, Sam, who is two, asks for Cheerios but—as soon as they're poured into a bowl with milk—he refuses them. *No! No! No! I want eggs! No Cheerios! Eggs!* Sam loves Cheerios, but he wants to see if Mom will make the eggs. Can you guess what happens?

Sam throws a fit. He shoves his bowl out of his reach. He starts crying with tears streaming down his face. When his mother moves the Cheerios bowl closer to Sam, he turns enraged. *No Cheerios! No Cheerios!* Red in the face, screaming, crying, and kicking, Sam is letting it all out—and he knows *exactly* what he is doing. And, without fail, Mom starts making the eggs. She doesn't want Sam to be hungry at preschool, and she is in a rush to get the older kids off to school. Sam calms down immediately. Just like in infancy, Sam's mother will do anything to stop the crying.

Now Sam knows he has more power than he thought. This is intoxicating, and Sam starts to find lots of other ways to get Mom to do his bidding. When she says no to a toy at CVS, Sam throws a giant tantrum. *He! Wants! His! Toy!* Mom is embarrassed. She feels the other shoppers turn their gaze to her son, and then to her, with *that* look. You know the look. It says, "You are a terrible parent, because if you were a good parent your child wouldn't act this way. Now shut that kid up." In no mood for a public power struggle, Mom buys the toy. Sam is thrilled. Not only does he have a new plastic robot thing, but he coerced Mom into doing what *he* wanted. Again. This behavior is really working out for him.

Not so much for Mom.

The cumulative effect of Sam's actions is a fairly consistent battle of wills. Mom or Dad say one thing. Sam says another. They say, "No!" He says, "Yes!" Sometimes Mom and Dad win the battle. Although they are drained from the experience, they leave the store without the toy. Over time, though, Sam wins the war. He isn't bothered by the constant negotiation. It is fun, it draws loads of attention, and it sometimes even produces a toy or an ice-cream cone. But Mom and Dad are beaten down by the ceaseless battle. They want "no" to mean "no." Can't they just run into the store without buying anything? Yes, they can.

But not until they change the dynamic.

Let's Negotiate

A few years ago, I did some mediation work. Divorced couples would meet me in a small office, arguing over schedules and visitation and such, and I'd try to broker a compromise. That's how mediation is supposed to work. If everyone gives a little, then everyone can win a little. That's the idea, at least. But in parenting, the reality is that once mothers and fathers negotiate with their children, they lose. Why? Because negotiation is almost always initiated by the child for the benefit of the child. Two examples illustrate this point.

Maddie wants a cookie, but her dad says no. Undeterred, Maddie asks, "If I eat all of my carrots, could I have a cookie for dessert?" Dad agrees, and Maddie eats the carrots. Maybe

Maddie would have eaten the carrots anyway. But even if she wouldn't have, she found a way to reverse her dad's decision. This negotiation was just the beginning for Maddie. Next week Maddie again tries to trade carrots for a cookie, but this time she learns to be more strategic. After her dad agrees to let her have a cookie if she eats her carrots, she asks, "Do I have to eat them all?" Dad says, "No, just have five." "How about two?" Maddie retorts. Dad says, "Four." Maddie says, "Three." Dad says, "Fine." Now any time Dad wants Maddie to do anything, she initiates mediation. Inevitably, she gains much more than she gives and Dad loses more than he gains.

Here's another example from Nancy's household. Nancy is a single mom raising two teenagers—Tommy, who is sixteen, and Alyssa, thirteen. Nancy tells Tommy it is time to turn off the Xbox. He has been playing for more than two hours, and it's bedtime. Tommy knows that even though his mom said he should put the game away, he really doesn't have to. At first Tommy just ignores his mom. That will get him a good fifteen to twenty minutes while she is busy with his sister before bed. Every now and then, Nancy yells for him to turn it off, but he doesn't listen. When Nancy comes back in the room, she says in a slightly more angry voice, "Tommy, turn it off!" This is when the negotiating begins. He says, "I can't right now. I am in the middle of the fill-in-the-blank-most-important-moment-of-the-game. Can't I just have ten more minutes? Then I'll get right in bed." Exasperated with this nightly ritual, Nancy walks out of the room saying, "Fine. Just ten more minutes." Nancy feels like she is being firm, but Tommy knows Nancy is easily persuaded.

The problem with negotiating with children is the back-and-forth never ends. One concession leads to another and another. Even when parents want to put their foot down, they still have to deal with the begging and pleading and whining. It is beyond wearing. After every ruling, kids think there is wiggle room (because there usually is). Whenever parents tell me their children don't accept the word "no," I know what has been going on: negotiation.

If You Do That Again, I Will Lose My Mind

In a previous scenario, Sam used attention-seeking behavior to get something he wanted. Sometimes kids do the same type of behavior but the payoff is entirely different. I remember when I was a child, my older sister, Leah, and I liked to egg each other on. We would sit in the backseat of the car and shove and prod and kick and poke. Eventually, the fussing would become so maddening, our mom or dad would turn around and scream, in *that* voice, "Stop touching each other!"

Then the fun began. I would stick my finger out and put it as close to my sister as I could without actually touching her. She would whine, "Mommmmm, Catherine's touching me." And I would smirk back, "No, I'm not." With one little motion, I could simultaneously annoy both my mother and my sister. This almost always ended badly for me. Either my sister would whack me or my mother would force me to sit on the floor of the car. So why did I do it? I'll come back to that in a minute.

Years ago, I conducted a seminar about sibling rivalry to a group of twenty parents. I often advise parents to look into their own childhoods and sibling dynamics to better understand their children's sibling relationships. Anyway, one dad (we can call him John) made a comment that I have never forgotten. He told the story of his large family. There were six kids, and, this being the 1970s and all, they were often left to fend for themselves. John got bored and used to pick on his little sister. He made fun of her in every way possible, and she would inevitably run to their mother and complain. Feeling a soft spot for the little girl, his mother would then call John in for a talk. His mom said something that repeatedly served as his siren call. "Why do you tease your sister so much?" she would say. "You know when you call her names it really hurts her feelings." John chuckled as he recalled this story. He knows, in hindsight, it was cruel and heartless and maybe even a bit sadistic. But Mom's words, in fact, provided the secret code to continue to drive his sister crazy. He went on to intentionally provoke her with ease for years.

John wasn't proud of this story. He felt ashamed and regretful for hurting his sister. But at the time, getting under his sister's skin and stealing his mother's focus, even for a brief period, was intoxicating. John usually got yelled at and sometimes punished, but that didn't stop him.

After hearing John's story and his revelation, I realized why I did that same annoying behavior to my sister and even to my mother. I was a kid who felt powerless, and I knew I would get a reaction. Sometimes, parents don't give kids the attention they feel they need or want. And, as I have mentioned, if they can't land attention the delightful way, they will get it any way they can. When a parent is visibly angered by a child's behavior, it serves as encouragement. I know that's hard to believe. But I assure you it's true.

Children put out the bait, and parents gobble it up. Then kids pull them in, hook, line, and sinker. Parents then wonder endlessly why the kids continue to aggravate them *on purpose*. John, Sam, and I deliberately set out to entice our parents to respond to us. We could, with a fair degree of certainty, predict the outcome.

My Kid Makes Me Crazy and Doesn't Seem to Even Realize It

While there are kids who provoke parents on purpose, there are others who do it quite naturally. Some of these children have special needs, such as autism or attention deficit hyperactivity disorder (ADHD). Others act just a little bit different from other children. These kids make a lot more noises that drive parents insane—such as humming, loud talking, imitation, and baby talk. They shift in their seats if parents can get them to sit down at all. Repetitively clumsy, they drop cups, plates, and forks at every meal. Tripping and ripping pants is common, too. Parents begin having a heightened awareness to these behaviors, and with each new offense they become more and more exasperated. Once parents reach this point of frustration, they try to stop the behavior at all costs.

Take Billy. He has been recently diagnosed with ADHD, and has spent years struggling to focus on his homework. Billy tends to wiggle around *a lot*, and he sometimes hums loudly. His parents, exasperated with his lack of focus, repeatedly reprimand him. "Billy, sit still!" "Billy, stop making those noises!" "Could you please sit facing forward?" "Stop bending your ruler!" "Chew with your mouth closed!" "Stop touching everything in the store and hurry up!" They assume all of those redirections would help Billy focus. They were wrong.

Billy's behavior didn't improve, and it couldn't have. Half the time he wasn't even aware of his actions. What Billy's parents didn't realize was not only were all of those comments distracting, the constant barrage of commands was eating away at Billy's self-esteem. Billy didn't even realize he was doing those behaviors, so when his parents admonished him incessantly, he felt like a failure.

Still, Ignore It!? I'm Not Convinced.

So now you know why your kids misbehave. They do it for attention. Any attention is better than no attention. Children have also learned that whining, crying, begging, and negotiating all give them something they want. And we know that what parents are doing in response to all of this undesirable behavior isn't working. Parents are punishing and giving timeouts, but the behavior continues. Parents are yelling, too, but that isn't working, either.

Parents try to correct unwanted behavior. When the correction doesn't work, they do it louder. In a nationally representative study, 90 percent of American parents admitted to harsh verbal discipline. This is equally true both for parents of toddlers and those with a teenager living at home. Parents usually yell at their children because they are exasperated and out of tools. But even when it is done in love and for the perceived benefit of the child, it doesn't work. Not only does repetitive verbal discipline increase depression in children, it also increases conduct problems. These are the very problems about which parents are yelling.

Most parents underestimate the effect yelling has on children and the parent-child relationship. When a parent flies off the handle, very often there is remorse followed by a healthy conversation. However, even in homes where there is a great deal of warmth and exhibited love, harsh verbal discipline still makes children feel more hostile toward their parents. Children who have these antagonistic feelings toward Mom and Dad are also more likely to exhibit behavior problems. A cycle is created where it isn't clear if the chicken or the egg came first, but it doesn't matter. Yelling as a form of discipline doesn't benefit anyone.

When the power differential between parents and children is unclear and discipline is ineffectual, parents start disciplining often. They become hypersensitive to annoying and attention-seeking behaviors. Nagging children to stop whining or begging them to get off the floor and stop throwing a tantrum is exhausting. Parents who are encouraged to begin ignoring some of these behaviors for the sake of having them occur less frequently feel intense relief to let go of the daily battle. They get permission to look the other way (on purpose), and they feel better. Parents begin to enjoy their kids more, and, funny enough, kids begin enjoying their parents more, too.

Insanity is colloquially defined as doing the same thing over and over again but expecting different results. If what you are doing isn't improving behavior, then maybe it makes sense to try something different. Maybe something really different. Say, for example, ignoring children who are being inappropriate. In the next chapter, I will show you how and why ignoring works.

Important Points to Remember

- When you negotiate, you lose even if you win something.
- Any attention, even negative, is still motivating to a child.
- Children have learned from a young age to whine, cry, and negotiate to get something wanted.
- Young children have no control over their lives, so they try to exert control whenever possible.
- Hyperparenting created a generation of "watch me, watch me, watch me" kids.

CHAPTER 2

Positive and Negative Reinforcement: The Basics

A person who has been punished is not thereby simply less inclined to behave in a given way; at best, he learns how to avoid punishment. —B. F. SKINNER

CHILDREN ARE MASTERS of two distinctly cunning skills. One is avoidance. The other is winning. They learn these abilities at a young age, and they work hard over the years to perfect them for optimal outcome. Parents are often unaware that their children are employing these talents. And yet, children are using them in broad daylight, in front of other people.

Jason hates baths. Every night feels like going to war just to clean him up for bed. Jason's mom thinks he has trouble with transitions, so she tries to warn him that bath time is approaching. She'll say, "Jason, in five minutes, we are going to head upstairs for your bath. Okay?" No answer. Jason's mom busies herself cleaning up after dinner and gives her son the one-minute warning. Literally, she shouts, "One-minute warning!" Jason hears his mom and ignores her. He *really* doesn't want to take a bath tonight. Or any night. From experience, Jason knows that every now and then he can delay and stall and stall and delay so that there isn't enough time for the bath. Jason is hoping this is one of those nights.

He starts running around the house. Jason's mom is tired. She is in no mood for this. So she tries to grab Jason. Each time she lunges for him, he giggles. She tries harder and darts behind him, swatting at his shirt. He's hysterical, loving this chase. Jason's mom can feel herself giving up. She starts to think about what they did today. *Really, is Jason that dirty?* In her head, the dialogue goes thusly: *Well, we didn't go to the park. The library is clean. We didn't have a playdate, and he actually ate dinner fairly neatly. Ugh, maybe he doesn't need a bath.* And with that, Jason's mom says, "Actually, Jason, I changed my mind. You don't have to take a bath. You aren't that dirty. Let's just go up and get changed. If you hurry, you will have time for an extra story." What? The plan actually worked? Jason is shocked—it wasn't even his best effort. He didn't even get to the fake tears. Jason is elated. Giddy. He immediately rushes up the stairs. Who doesn't love an extra story?

While Jason is an expert at avoidance, Sonya's particular skill involves acquiring something special. Sonya is kind of a collector. She just likes stuff. She especially likes little toys— erasers, PEZ dispensers, stuffed animals for her backpack, super-bouncy balls. Really, anything that lights up. She's been working on a Pokémon collection. Lately, she has also eyed lip glosses of myriad flavors. If you asked Sonya's parents, they would tell you they rarely buy Sonya toys. Well, not for no reason. If Sonya behaves in the store, she might get a little something at the checkout counter. When Sonya sits quietly in the back of the car when her mom has an important phone call for work, Sonya knows she can usually count on an ice cream or a cookie. Today, when Sonya's mom decided to run into Toys "R" Us to get a gift for a neighbor's birthday party, Sonya brought forth her Academy Award–worthy A-game.

> Sonya: *Mom, can I get a new pack of Shopkins?*
> Mom: *No.*
> Sonya: *Why?*
> Mom: *Because you have enough.*
> Sonya: *Yeah, but I don't have any from Season Four. No one wants to trade with me anymore.*
> Mom: *That's ridiculous. I saw you trading with your brother yesterday.*
> Sonya: *Mommmmm!!!! That's because he doesn't know what are the good ones. Please . . .*
> Mom: *[Silence.]*
> Sonya: *Mom. Mom? MOM! Pleassseee. Just one pack. I promise I won't ask for any more after this.*
> Mom: *[Silence.]*
> Sonya: *Pleasssseee. Why can't I just get one pack?*
> Mom: *Okay, whatever. Pick out something for less than $10. But hurry up because we have to go.*
> Sonya: *Great. I will. Thank you so much, Mommy.*

Jason's special skill is used to avoid something objectionable. Acting out in this manner has helped Jason worm his way out of all sorts of things. Sonya whines, begs, pleads, and generally takes advantage of her parents to obtain stuff she wants. The most proficient of children learn how to use both of these skills interchangeably at will. These behaviors make parenting a lot less fun.

Why can't kids just take the bath without an argument? It is something done nearly every day. And why can't kids stop asking for stuff they don't even need? Why can't "no" be "no"? Why does everything have to be a negotiation? These questions can easily be answered by understanding positive and negative reinforcement. These are two frequently cited but regularly misunderstood concepts, and they are at the heart of Ignore it!. Chapter 2 will be devoted to helping you understand the why of children's behavior. Once you understand the why, changing the behavior becomes as simple as A-B-C.

Behavior Modification Is Not Just for Research

Burrhus Frederic (B. F.) Skinner, the famous psychologist, thought the key to understanding *why* people do what they do is to understand *what* they get from it. The kinds of incentives people receive are attention, material items, or getting out of undesirable requirements. Skinner believed that what happened immediately following an action would determine if that action would be repeated.

Take Sonya, for example. She has asked her mother before for a toy in the store, and her mother has said yes. Without knowing it, Sonya's mother reinforced Sonya's behavior and ensured that next time Sonya is in a store she will try to land a toy. Because, why not? Sonya's pleading worked once, so it is likely to work again. Sonya gets it intuitively.

Behavior that is reinforced in some way is likely to be

repeated. Think about synonyms for the word "reinforce": "emphasize," "strengthen," "buttress," "underpin," and "fortify." Clearly, reinforcing something makes it stronger. So what if you are reinforcing the wrong actions? This is the crux of understanding why children misbehave. Most typically, developing children really aren't to blame for their behavior. We, *the parents*, are responsible. That is actually good news. If we are responsible, we can also fix the problem by changing our own behavior. But let's not get ahead of ourselves. Let me first explain more about how positive and negative reinforcement works.

I'm a person with strong faith in the scientific method. If something cannot be observed and tested, I am skeptical. People used to believe the world was flat until science proved we lived on an enormous floating ball. The scientific method is a way of analyzing a theory by creating experiments to test a hypothesis. I need science behind my work. Yes, I have practice wisdom based on years of experience working with families and children. But without the science to back up my work, I wouldn't be able to see whether my interventions were working. I like to know the most efficient and effective ways to improve children's behavior.

I digress. Back to Skinner . . .

Skinner's theory about how behavior is learned is called "operant conditioning." To test his hypothesis, Skinner designed several experiments. He used rats and pigeons in his experiments. But in my work as a family coach, I have seen all of the same processes in children. Although it doesn't always seem as such, our offspring are born a blank slate in terms of behavior. They are not wise to the ways of the world. However, as I described in Chapter 1, newborn babies quickly learn that crying is immediately followed by a parent meeting their needs. The parent's behavior greatly influences how the baby will try to get his needs met again.

In any given situation, there is something that happens before the behavior (*A* for "Antecedent"), during the behavior (*B* for "Behavior"), and as a result of the behavior (*C* for "Consequence"). Here is an example of A-B-C: Meghan's dad takes Meghan to visit Grandma in the nursing home (Antecedent). Five-year-old Meghan hates visiting Grandma because the nursing home is dreary and smells like moldy pears. As soon as the family arrives at the nursing home, Meghan starts acting out (Behavior). She is throwing toys around the visiting room, screaming obnoxiously, stealing soap from the bathroom. Dad says, "Meghan, if you don't stop this behavior, we are going to have to leave. You don't want to upset Grandma, do you?"

Um, that's *exactly* what Meghan wants. She's a little kid who really has no beef with Grandma, but would rather be anywhere but here. Meghan keeps up the pressure. She's whining, yelling, tugging, griping. The looks are piercing. An old woman mumbles, "What a monster," under her breath. It's beyond awkward, and not twenty-five minutes after seeing Grandma, the family says their good-byes and insufferable Meghan wins again (Consequence). So what motivates the child? Meghan's father's admission that acting out would result in their departure was exactly what helped her decide on her behavior. Guess what is likely to happen next time they go to visit Grandma? If Meghan is on her game, she'll start the obnoxious behavior before even departing the house. Eventually, Dad will decide to leave Meghan at home altogether. Mission accomplished!

A-B-C Basics

A: **Antecedent:** The trigger that prompts the behavior
B: **Behavior:** Whining, complaining, negotiating, yelling, crying, tantrums
C: **Consequence:** Positive (obtaining something or avoiding of something) or negative (getting yelled at, punished)

The consequence is the most telling reason why children act in a certain manner. Consequences have a somewhat negative connotation, but in truth it is just the result or effect of an action. Consequences can be positive. For example, I recently made brownies for a new neighbor. As a consequence of my actions, the neighbors invited me in to meet their daughter and dog and see their home. This exchange promoted a new relationship as a consequence of my actions (baking brownies). The situation played out so beautifully that when new neighbors move into a house that's for sale on my street, I will, without fail, bring them brownies, too. Consequences control whether a behavior will be seen again and how often. I will discuss how to use consequences to improve behavior in greater detail in Chapter 10.

Using the Antecedent-Behavior-Consequence model, let's review a few of the scenarios that I presented in this chapter so far. Jason wants to avoid the bath, Sonya wants a toy, and Meghan doesn't want to visit the nursing home.

Scenario	Antecedent	Behavior	Consequence	What Is learned?
Jason needs a bath.	Mom tells Jason it's time for his bath.	Running around the house	Mom decides to give up the bath for the night.	Jason can avoid something he doesn't want to do by disobeying.
Sonya and her mom head to the toy store.	Being in a toy store	Whining and nagging for new toy	Mom buys the toy.	Getting a toy is easy and whining is an effective tool.
Meghan visits her grandma.	Being in the dreary nursing home	Acting out, such as throwing toys	Dad decides to leave.	Bad behavior will exclude Meghan from undesirable family outings.

Meghan and Jason both want to avoid something, while Sonya wants to get something. This is the difference between positive and negative reinforcement. In positive reinforcement (like what was provided to Sonya), the behavior is reinforced by giving something. What is given can be enjoyable (more dessert, toy, positive attention) or unpleasant (screaming, berating, negative attention). On the other hand, Meghan and Jason experience negative reinforcement. Many parents incorrectly think of negative reinforcement as providing something unpleasant, which thus stops the behavior. For example, yelling at a child to stop hitting a sibling. Well, this is actually still positive reinforcement. The yelling provides attention, and that can be enough to reinforce the behavior. Negative reinforcement is simply taking away something undesirable after the behavior. For Jason, taking away the bath negatively reinforced his behavior, and Meghan got out of visiting her grandmother. The behaviors happened, and they prompted the parents to take something away. Without knowing it, both parents ensured their children will continue with the exact same behavior.

Positive reinforcement: Behavior is encouraged by offering something desirable (attention, food, or toys).
Negative reinforcement: Behavior is encouraged by simply taking away something undesirable.

Before moving on, take some time to consider your children and some of their most troubling behaviors. Try to find at least four examples of undesirable behavior for each child and fill out the chart* below. It might be helpful to jot down A-B-C on a piece of paper and keep it with you for a few days. Every time one of your children whines or tantrums or acts out in some way, try to include that scenario on the chart. Taking the time to do this step is very important. You will be able to use this information when we go over the steps for Ignore it!. Remember that the consequences are the benefits of the behavior. It will also be important to know the function of the behavior when we talk about how to reward good behavior in Chapter 9.

Scenario with Time and Location	Antecedent	Behavior	Consequence	What Is Learned?

*Additional chart with more space can be found in Appendix C. A customizable chart is available at www.TheFamilyCoach.com.

When trying to assess behavior, it can be helpful to ask a few questions to clarify the issues. To begin with, find out when and where the behavior usually occurs. A mom called recently, seeking help with her five-year-old daughter in the mornings. The girl refuses to get dressed. When did this happen? In the morning. Where? In the daughter's room. Knowing these trigger times and locations will help mom ignore the acting-out behavior in the future. Sometimes, kids act up for just certain family members. If this is the case, note who is usually present during the behavior.

For example, in one particular household dad is a softy. He gets upset whenever his daughter cries (even if it's during a tantrum). He usually tries to make her feel better with a hug. But the attention and affection in that moment simply guarantee that his daughter will continue to use crying to her advantage. So in this case, the behavior happens when Dad is around. Other children are perfect angels until a sibling shows up. You may also want to ask yourself if there are certain activities that precede the attention-seeking or negative behavior. Sometimes children have a difficult transition from parent to babysitter or from sitter back to parent. These transitions can bring about the problematic behavior.

My children historically behave the worst right after a visit to Grandma and Grandpa's home. They are whinier, and they complain much more. In fairness, it's not that the grandparents are a problem per se. It's just that their rules are drastically different from ours. The kids get away with a lot more, as they should when with their grandparents. But man, can reentry be rough while the kids get adjusted back into our house.

I Still Don't Know Why I Should Ignore It!

Changing behavior is simple. I promise. All you have to do is eliminate the benefit (consequence) and the behavior just disappears. Poof! Gone! Seriously, it's that simple. Truly, it is. When I lay out how to change behavior for parents in my practice, they very often say, "That won't work," or, "I tried that already." So if variations of those words are circulating through your head, well, you're not the first, and you're not alone. But you're wrong. In my private practice, doubting parents have already paid for my services, so they go ahead and—doubts be damned—give it a try. And you know what? They usually admit afterward that their skepticism was misguided.

As I laid out in the previous section, behavior that is rewarded in some way, even if it isn't the most ideal reward, is more likely to be repeated. Luckily, not *all* behavior is repeated. Ineffective ways of acting almost miraculously disappear. If a parent doesn't reinforce a child's behavior, it fades away or, at the bare minimum, drastically wanes. When nothing is gained and nothing is avoided, children naturally find other ways to act. If running around the house did not help Jason avoid taking a bath, he wouldn't do it. If begging and whining didn't help Sonya get a new toy, she wouldn't bother, either. That's because children (and parents and dogs and cats and even rats) don't want to waste time doing something that will not yield the desired result. If a behavior doesn't serve a purpose, we let it go. This is the idea behind extinction.

Extinction: The process of eliminating or reducing a conditioned response by not reinforcing it.

The concept of extinction is defined as the process of eliminating or reducing a conditioned response by not reinforcing it. What does this even mean? Well, conditioning is just what kids have learned over time. Children act and parents respond. When this process happens over and over again, children become conditioned (think Pavlov's dogs here). However, when the response changes, the behavior also changes. When parents stop responding to inappropriate behavior in the typical way they have been, the behavior becomes extinct. "Extinction" literally means dying out or vanishing.

Back when I was a little girl, my older sister, Leah, used to harass me by calling me big words from the dictionary. Maybe it's a peculiar method of taunting, but it's effective. It worked *every* time. With each "Your protoplasm is subpar" or "You're so facetious," I'd go running to my mother, screaming, "Leah just called me a facetious again!" I had no idea what any of it meant. My sister loved how she could get to me. I annoyed my sister (Antecedent), she called me big SAT words (Behavior), and I reinforced it by hollering each time (Consequence). Eventually, I grew up and learned how to use a dictionary. My sister's big words ceased having an effect on me, so she stopped using them. The behavior was eradicated.

Here is another example. A mom I know hates when her daughter—in need of something—shouts from another room. I asked her what she did when her daughter yelled. The mom said she yelled back. I told my friend that her daughter was yelling because, each and every time, my friend responded. I asked her to simply ignore her daughter when she yells from another room. She should simply pretend she doesn't hear unless her daughter is in the same room or the house is on fire.

My friend initially balked because she didn't think she could tolerate the yelling. But I asked her to give it a try. So the next time her daughter yelled, she ignored it. The daughter assumed Mom didn't hear her, and yelled louder. Then louder still. Eventually, the daughter showed up in the same room as her mom and said, "Mom, didn't you hear me?" My friend smiled and said, "Yes, I heard you. But you know I don't like it if you yell from the other room. Thank you for finding me. Now how can I help you?" And that was that. The daughter continued to yell across the house for a few days, but when she failed to evoke a response, she eventually quit doing it. I mean, who wants to yell and scream across the house if it doesn't get anyone's attention?

I hesitate to bring this back to the animal world, but I'd like to offer one more example. When my family brought home our now-beloved dog, Norma, we decided to crate-train her. At night, Norma was to be put in her crate (cage) to sleep until the morning. This process helps prevent potty accidents because dogs don't like to excrete where they sleep. (For the record, neither do I.) Anyway, when we first put Norma in her crate at night, she was not pleased. She scratched at the gate. She cried. Barked. This broke our hearts. So every time I heard it I would head down to the crate and tap it loudly to show Norma that I didn't appreciate her making such a racket. But the action didn't work. Norma didn't stop because she liked to see me come to the crate—*even though I was making an unpleasant noise.* Eventually,

I got so tired of running up and down the stairs to admonish my dog that I simply ignored her. Norma is no dummy, and she soon realized that I wasn't coming back. After a short period, she stopped crying and went to sleep. The next night, she again whined and pouted when we put her in her crate. But this time I ignored her noises, and she stopped after a few minutes. By the third night, she stopped yelping about the crate. And she started loving that crate. If the door was open during the day, we would often find her lounging in there. This is a perfect example of extinction. I was reinforcing Norma's behavior every time I gave her attention, even though I was angry and not particularly nice. When I withdrew my attention and ignored her behavior, even the dog realized there is no point to continue with it. I assure you, your child is more intelligent than my dog.

So why did I have to bring Norma into this discussion? Because I wanted to make the point that this process, if followed consistently, always yields the same outcome—the behavior is eliminated. That's it. So if you have been offering attention to your child throwing a giant tantrum (because she wanted pink socks even though she said she wanted the purple ones), withholding all attention will make that tantrum a lot less rewarding. If you ignore it, the child won't get an opportunity to change socks and won't get thirty minutes of negotiating. That tantrum really starts to feel useless.

Before moving on, I just want to review a few really important points from this chapter.

1. Behavior that is reinforced is repeated.
2. Behavior that evokes a negative response is still repeated because any attention is a reward.

3. There are two main motivations for behavior: to obtain something or to avoid something.
4. Behavior that is not reinforced (or is ignored) wanes.

When I go into a home to observe a family, I like to blend in with the furniture. I try not to engage in the family dynamics because I want to see what is really going on. Kids quickly forget I'm there because I can sometimes even be in another room listening. During the initial phone consultation, I ask parents to tell me some of the most difficult times with their children. Topping the list are, without fail, mornings and the hours between four p.m. and dinnertime. I tend to visit at these times. Inevitably, I see the same dynamics but in different houses. By the time dinner rolls around, many parents are done. I mean *done* done. Toast. Exhausted. Wiped out. In no mood for kids who don't listen. Many have already worked a long day. Others are beaten down from the solitude of caring for children alone, sans help or relief. This is the witching hour. So what do I observe? Yelling. A lot of yelling. When there isn't yelling, there is often something equally unwanted—sarcasm. Some parents turn to mocking, and even cruelty, without knowing it because they are frustrated by the lack of listening and the acting-out behaviors. Last, some parents just give up. They almost stop parenting and give in to their kids' demands because they just can't fight it all the time. "Fine, watch *The Hunger Games*." "Fine, play a video game where the goal is to assassinate a coke-running murderous dictator." "Fine, use the Taser on your sister." Ignore it! eliminates yelling. It abolishes negotiating. Ignore it! wipes out the need to surrender. If you are prone to raising your voice or to becoming a teeny bit grumpy, or if you have ever given up on what you know is right as a parent because you were beaten down, Ignore it! will change your life.

How long will this miracle take to work? No time at all. Usually children who are not reinforced stop their behavior within a few days. *Wait . . . what?* Yes, a few days. Imagine that there are two routes you can take to school for pickup. One way is always crammed with traffic and has a lot of lights. The other way is a little longer, but there is never any traffic, and it turns out to be faster. How long do you think it would take you to decide not to take the light-filled, traffic-loaded way? Not long at all. The same is true for Ignore it!.

Now you are ready to learn how to actually do the ignoring. Let's get to work. . . .

The concept of extinction and behavior modification was used in an interesting study about bullying. Since bullying is often reinforced by peers, researchers created an antibullying program that eliminated the social attention benefit for the bully. The hypothesis was that bullying would decrease when teachers and students did not reinforce the behavior. The school community was taught not to whine, complain, cheer, or laugh at all when they saw bullying behavior (e.g., complaining or whining on the part of the victim, and cheering or laughing on the part of bystanders) following disrespectful behavior. Instead, students were taught to recognize the behavior as bullying, hold a hand up, say "no," and then simply walk away. Bystanders were taught the same technique but were told to help the target of the bullying to walk away. Amazing results were observed. Bullying decreased and so did bystander support of bullying. Same concepts applied in a different setting. Ignore it! works.

ıllıllıllıllıllıllıllıllıllıllıllıllıllıllıllıllıllıllıllıllıllıllıllıllıllıllıllıllıllıllıllıllıllıllıllıllıllıllıllıllıllıll

Important Points to Remember

- Behavior that is reinforced in any way is likely to be repeated.
- Extinction is the process of eliminating or reducing a conditioned response by not reinforcing it.
- When the response to the behavior changes, the behavior also changes.

CHAPTER 3

Ignore What?

KNOW YOU ARE raring to begin ignoring your children, and I don't blame you. I'm excited for you, too. But before you start, I want to make clear what *can*—and what should *never*—be ignored. Many annoying and frustrating behaviors should be ignored. But this book is not an invitation to put your feet up and read *Us Weekly* while your kids are playing in traffic. Ignore it! teaches the concept of selective ignoring. Parents only look like they are ignoring the child. In reality, they are very much tuned in with what the child is doing. As soon as the child changes the behavior, the parent begins to immediately reengage. You will learn this in Chapter 4.

Over the years in practice, I have found that parents are very eager to make changes to improve family life. However, their interventions frequently fail to make the desired alteration. When I offer suggestions, parents regularly tell me, "Oh, I tried that already. It didn't work." They aren't lying. They did honestly make an attempt to implement a technique they read about or learned somewhere. Where they collapse is in the details. When working with a family, I generally follow up a consultation with two weeks of daily phone or e-mail contact. I do this because there is often a learning curve to implementing a new technique. Typically, there is a moment of truth, a moment when the technique is put to the test. At that point in time, parents turn flustered and sometimes make choices that undo all of their hard work and good intentions. Just a little more preparation or support would have prevented that mistake.

Because there is so much more you can ignore, it actually makes sense to kick off with what you cannot. We can only ignore behavior that is produced as a direct result of our reinforcement. When we provide a benefit for an action, it is likely to be repeated. Conversely, a behavior that has not been reinforced or has no perceived benefit is *not* likely to be repeated. That's the basis for extinction. However, there are some behaviors that occur naturally without any kind of reinforcement. In these cases, there is no advantage to ignoring, but there could be some potential downsides. One example of this is crying from pain or fear. Not all crying is equal. Crocodile tears (an insincere show of emotion) are not what I'm talking about here. You can go ahead and ignore that dramatic show of quasi-emotion. The kind of crying you cannot ignore is when it is a response to genuine pain. Pain can be physical or emotional, and it is unwise to ignore either. A true show of emotion is not produced in response to a previous reinforcement, so ignoring it is inappropriate. (There is an exception to this, but I will save that for another section of this book.)

In most of the examples I have presented thus far in this book, a parent is providing the benefit for the child's behavior. A parent gives the wanted attention. A begging and, frankly, annoying child convinces a parent to buy a toy. However, sometimes children exhibit behavior that is not rewarded by the parent. The reward is internal for the child. For example, overeating. Children (and, yes, adults too) often overeat because they are benefiting from the actual food. Instead of feeling emotions, people eat. Instead of listening to one's body when full, people still eat. Most overeaters are not doing it because a parent or friend is giving attention or rewarding the overeating. Therefore, ignoring the problem will not solve the problem. Any activity or behavior that has an internal reward should not be ignored.

In addition to not ignoring internally rewarding behavior, parents should not ignore behaviors that have a goal to be left alone. Take the example of a child who wants a cookie. Child asks for a cookie. Parent says no to the cookie. Next time, the child thinks that instead of asking and being denied, it might be better just to take the cookie. This is a sneaky behavior and it shouldn't be ignored. Ignoring sneakiness only encourages the behavior to continue. Getting away with it can also be its own internal reward.

Behaviors that are illegal should also not be ignored. Vandalism, stealing, or battery all need to be addressed carefully. Children who exhibit dangerous outbursts that include extreme violence must also not be ignored. This is true also for children who are abusive toward siblings. Not only is the reaction from the sibling the reinforcer, but it is unethical to look the other way while a child is being physically harmed. If you have a child who is exhibiting any of these behaviors, I recommend seeking treatment from a mental health professional in your area. Behavior modification as described in this book may still be appropriate. But treatment is safer and more successful if monitored by a specialist.

Ignore it! is successfully used with children who have a wide range of developmental disabilities and mental health diagnoses, including autism and attention deficit hyperactivity disorder. However, children who exhibit self-injurious behavior need a special kind of intervention to prevent excessive self-harm. Children who cut, headbang, use excessive force, bite, or scratch may do so for a variety of reasons. If the reason is for social attention, this program may help. However, due to the many other reasons (managing pain, self-soothing, frustration, or sensory deficits), it would be unwise to ignore the behavior without a careful analysis of the root causes.

There is one more type of behavior that parents shouldn't ignore. When I observe a family, I almost always find that parents offer far more corrective attention (stop, no, don't) and nagging than they offer positive feedback for good behavior. The problem isn't that kids are just acting up way more than they are behaving. It is more that the squeaky wheel gets the grease. Unfortunately, sometimes parents unknowingly practice unintentional extinction. Remember that removing the benefits of the behavior causes the behavior to cease to exist. So far I've mostly discussed providing children with negative attention for their inappropriate or undesirable behaviors. But parents frequently withhold positive reinforcement when a child performs a very desirable behavior. This isn't premeditated or on purpose. It just happens. Without persistent positive feedback, children sometimes decide that performing undesirable tasks (taking out trash, cleaning up room, using good manners) aren't worth it, and they just stop doing them. This book will teach you to reintroduce positive reinforcement for the behaviors you *want* to see after learning how to withdraw reinforcement for the behavior you don't.

Finally, What You Can Ignore

If I asked a bunch of parents to list the top five behaviors children do that absolutely drive them insane, most would be unable to contain themselves. Just five? How about ten, eleven, twelve, thirty, forty? Generally, the behaviors on this list are the ones you can ignore. For example, making annoying noises . . .

BLEEEEEEP.
BOOOPY.
BOOOOBY.
SHLOPSCHUP.
MEMEMEMEMEMEM.
HMMMMMMMMM.
LALALALALALAL
HIPPIE YIPPIE KAJIPPIE MAPIPPIE FLADIPPY

Imagine these awkward combinations of letters being uttered in the most hair-raising, nails-on-a-chalkboard kind of way. Chances are, if you heard such an annoying word or noise, you would immediately snap and bark, "Stop saying that! It's annoying!" Bingo! Your kid immediately realizes this stuff works. And so it begins. Any useless or annoying noise, excessive humming, whistling, and baby talk can be ignored.

Scratch that. Anything that is annoying *must* be ignored. There are two reasons you can ignore these behaviors. To start with, if they are attention-seeking in nature (meaning that the purpose is to get a reaction), then ignoring will eliminate the benefit. That's classic extinction. The other reason to Ignore it! is that if your children are annoying without even knowing it, then you aren't reinforcing them with your attention. All you would be doing if you reprimand is to push a child's self-esteem lower for something he doesn't even know he is doing. There is no benefit to the child or to the parent, so ignore it all.

Do you have a little drama queen or king? You know, the ones who blow everything out of proportion? Everything is important and an emergency. Melodrama reigns. One minute they are starving or dying and the next minute they run off playing happily. They cry and complain loudly (and often), and their reactions are unreasonably out of proportion. A minor cut or bruise required *loads* of attention and Band-Aids and ice packs. When something doesn't go the way of the dramatic child, he starts with the "No one loves me" or "You are so mean to me" and, quite possibly, the ol' "I'm going to die." Drama queens and kings use emotions to manipulate parents to do what they want. Parents try to avoid the bloodcurdling meltdowns by preemptively organizing around a child's desires or giving in (often after saying no). You've already learned that saying no but then yes only teaches kids to push until they score the desired answer. If you have a dramatic child, you now have permission to ignore this type of behavior. Anything overblown, out of proportion, or dramatic can be ignored.

Whining is another superpower possessed by children. It tends to begin right after a child is given a directive (e.g., "clean your room") or immediately following a request being turned down. The sound for each child is different, but generally it's complaining that is presented in that long, high-pitched dreadful way. The sole purpose of whining is to wear parents down. Kids only whine because it is functional. It works like a charm. It doesn't matter if it only works sporadically. That's called intermittent reinforcement, and it's still reinforcement. However, the result of intermittent reinforcement produces behavior that occurs at a higher rate and is more resistant to extinction than behavior that has been continuously reinforced. Even when children don't earn the desired outcome when they whine, they still garner attention. Negotiation works the exact same way. So ignore any whining, negotiating, or complaining presented by your child.

Intermittent reinforcement refers to behavior that is only sporadically reinforced. Children learn that sometimes their behavior produces the desired outcome. Even if sometimes their behavior doesn't produce the desired result, there is hope that sometimes it will. Thus, behavior that is reinforced intermittently is more resistant to change.

A battle of wills is like United States–Russia negotiation. Both sides dig in their heels and become steeled to win at all costs. Teens are notoriously good at this battle. Their tenacity and fortitude cannot be rivaled. However, toddlers use their irrationality on their side in the battle. It doesn't matter what the age of the child, the battle of wills cannot be won by any-one. Once a parent enters the arguing arena, attention is being paid to this behavior. Thus, whenever there is a dispute, you can bet this type of battle will rear its head. Additionally, it is ex-hausting to argue, and hurtful words can be said. Instead of joining the battle, ignore all attempts to engage. Nagging is another way to not take "no" for an answer. Ignore pestering, badgering, or any begging that is done to make you change your mind about anything.

I mentioned earlier that you cannot ignore crying that results from real or emotional pain. However, you can—and definitely should—ignore all insincere crying. How can you spot fake emotion? Well, crying that has no tears is a good place to start. Look for crying that intensifies when someone is watching or engaging. Children calm down, but as soon as an adult (who can be manipulated) walks near, the hysterics return. Ignore it all. Once the child is calm, you can still discuss any real underlying emotions—but don't give the phony tears any at-tention.

Some kids are keenly aware of their parents' soft spots or nerves. For example, I'm acquainted with a mother who cannot tolerate disrespectful children. Any backtalk puts her over the edge. Her sons know this and use it to aggravate her. Some kids use curse words. Others say mean or offensive things for the sole purpose of hurting the parent.

"You are fat and ugly and no one will love you. Ever!"

"Your cooking sucks."

"I hate you and so does everyone else."

"You are the meanest dad in the world."

These comments injure even if one understands that the child might not actually mean the stated sentiment. We all have insecurities, and when children exploit those, it is painful. It is almost impossible not to react. But you can't. You have to ignore all cursing, shocking statements, and disrespect when it is done for the purpose of hurting you.

Google the word "tantrums" and more than 19,700,000 entries are available. Due to an increased focus and knowledge about tantrums, some parents are learning to ignore them better. However, from my experience most parents don't ignore *all* tantrums (hence, that intermittent reinforcement again). Tantrums that happen in public, like in line at Trader Joe's or for a drink at Starbucks, are tougher to ignore. But for every reaction to the tantrum, kids only learn to use the outbursts as reliable methods to gain what they desire. All tantrums should be handled with Ignore it!.

This next one might be the most difficult of all to ignore. It is hard for me to even write about it because, just being honest, I struggle with the mental visuals. It's throwing up on command. Some kids have this ability, and it is an endgame for most parents. These children aren't sick. They have a pattern of using vomiting as a form of manipulation. It might have started by accident from an excessive tantrum. But when a parent runs to the child, calls off the dispute, and resolves the situation favorably for the child, the behavior quickly morphs into a pattern. Don't give in and do ignore vomiting on command. When the child calms down, you can clean up. The key to ignoring it is not reacting at all. This will be emphasized in Chapter 4, but I just wanted to clarify here.

A summary of what to ignore and what not to ignore is listed below. However, in Chapter 4 I will help you identify specific behaviors that you will want to ignore with your children.

What to Ignore	What Not to Ignore
Insincere crying (or crying with no tears)	Vandalism
Tantrums	Stealing
Shocking statements	Sneaky behaviors
Cursing for attention	Crying from fear, pain, emotional distress
Throwing up on command	Extreme and dangerous behavior
Whining	Behavior where being left alone is desirable
Nagging	Self-injurious behavior
Pestering	Overeating
Begging	Criminal behavior
Negotiating	Good and appropriate behavior
Attention-seeking behaviors	
Disrespectful comments	
Battle of wills	

Important Points to Remember

- Only ignore behavior that is produced as a direct result of your reinforcement.
- Any activity or behavior that has an internal reward should not be ignored.
- Do not ignore behaviors when your child is acting out to force you to leave him or her alone.

- Behavior that is illegal or poses danger to a child or someone else should not be ignored.
- Anything that is annoying *must* be ignored.
- Anything overblown, out of proportion, or dramatic can be ignored, as well as all insincere crying.

PART II

CHAPTER 4

How Do I Get Started?

A MY IS ABOUT to drive her two boys to a birthday party. When she turns on the car, she hears her favorite song: Elton John's "Mona Lisa and Mad Hatters." She explains to the children that it's a tune she absolutely loves. "When it's over," she says, "I'll get the Kidz Bop going for you." She is trying to teach her kids that the radio is for everyone. Nary a second after the words escape her lips, Charlie (her older) brings forth the whining: "But whhhhhyyyyyy do we have to waaaaaiiiit?" he wails. Amy—calm as can be—says, "Because I love this song, and I am listening to the end of it." Charlie has none of it. "Ugh!" he growls. "This song is horrible! Turn! It! Off!" The back-and-forth continues until halfway through the song Amy can't take it anymore. She turns to Charlie and furiously says, "Fine. Here's your music. Happy?" Amy mutters a string of nasty words beneath her breath while turning up an awful Kidz Bop rendition of Shawn Mendes's "Stitches" and sinks into her seat. She feels like a deflated punching bag.

Charlie, meanwhile, smiles widely. He has won, and they both know it.

Now here's how that car ride would go when Amy learns to Ignore it!.

Amy is about to drive her two boys to a birthday party. When she turns on the car, she hears her favorite song: Elton John's "Mona Lisa and Mad Hatters." She explains to the children that it's a tune she absolutely loves. "When it's over," she says, "I'll get the Kidz Bop going for you." She is trying to teach her kids that the radio is for everyone. Nary a second after the words escape her lips, Charlie (her older) brings forth the whining: "But whhhhhyyyyyy do we have to waaaaaiiiit?" he wails. Amy says nothing and ignores Charlie, because she already explained the plan. "Why can't we listen now?" he asks. Amy hears Charlie, but is contentedly ignoring him. This is her jam, and she's singing along in her head. "Ugh!" he growls. "This song is horrible! Turn! It! Off!" Amy focuses on the song, not Charlie. Resigned, he sits quietly. When the song finishes, Charlie asks, "So now will you put on our music?" Amy says, "Sure." She turns on Kidz Bop, and Charlie sits back and smiles happily while singing away to a rendition of Shawn Mendes's "Stitches." Amy smiles, too, because she knows Charlie just learned that arguing and complaining will not make her deviate from her plan. The next time they're in the car, Amy tells the boys she will change the station after her song wraps. Charlie nods and plays with his brother. It's a nonissue.

The first few chapters of this book set the stage for selective ignoring. There are several reasons why it is important for you to grasp the philosophy behind the technique before moving ahead to learning the process. As you read in Chapter 3, there are a number of occasions when one should not ignore behavior. It is never a good idea to ignore a child who is hurt or scared. You shouldn't turn your back on your child when he has a developmental disability that would make it difficult for him to understand your behavior. And you should never ignore your child when it could put him or someone else in danger. Being clear on these rules will give you confidence to ignore with full resolve when it is appropriate.

Learning what not to ignore is a vital lesson. However, learning what you *can* ignore is much more exciting (yes, exciting!). In Chapter 3, you learned that you can ignore annoying behaviors like loud talking, pencil tapping, and nudging. You can also ignore attention-seeking behavior such as whining, negotiating, and complaining. Ah, this is where the magic begins.

There is another important reason why you need to be clear on the principles behind ignoring. When you are pretending not to see your six-year-old twins begging for a pack of Bubblicious while checking out at the supermarket, some of the other customers might give you the evil eye. They are almost certainly thinking to themselves, *Just buy the darn gum so the annoying kids shut up.*

But—stares and awkward whispering be damned—making the purchase at that moment will only reinforce the kids' bad behavior and ensure that it will rear its ugly head again and again. And you will hold your head high knowing you are practicing behavior modification, which is a well-researched training method that has been used successfully for decades.

||||||||||||||||||||||||||||||||||||||||||||||||||||||||||||||||||||||||||||||||||||||||||||||||||||||||||||||||||||||||||||||||||||||||||||||||||

Behavior modification is the systematic application of principles and techniques to assess and improve behaviors.

||||||||||||||||||||||||||||||||||||||||||||||||||||||||||||||||||||||||||||||||||||||||||||||||||||||||||||||||||||||||||||||||||||||||||||||||||

In this chapter I will help you identify where to begin. It is a good idea to start with a few triggers (ways your children get to you) so you can stay focused and not ignore everything. You will learn to evaluate how you have been responding to a variety of behaviors and why they have been ineffective. Once you are clear on what you will ignore, I will teach you the process of selective ignoring. By the end of this chapter, you will be armed with the information you need, and you can start ignoring. The rest of the book will help you be optimally effective, and show you how to troubleshoot if you are not seeing immediate improvement. You will also learn how to encourage desirable behaviors.

There are six steps I will review in this chapter:

Step One: Observe
Step Two: Create a list of target behaviors
Step Three: Ignore
Step Four: Listen
Step Five: Reengage
Step Six: Repair

Steps one and two are only necessary when beginning this program for the first time. They will put you in the most ideal mind-set to start ignoring. If at any point you get sidetracked or stop ignoring and want to begin again, review and complete these steps. Steps three through six are what you will actually do each and every time you Ignore It!. The steps are Ignore, Listen, Reengage, and Repair. I will review all of these steps in great detail in the rest of this chapter.

As a way to easily remember steps three through six, I want you to think of the sentence "I Like Relaxed Reading." This sentence serves two purposes. The first two letters of each word (except "I") correspond to the first letters of the steps in order. "I" for Ignore. The "Li" in "like" is for **Li**sten. The "Re" in "relaxed" is for **Re**engage, and the "Re" in "reading" is for **Re**pair. This will help you remember what to do.

I also very purposely used the word "relaxed" to remind you that in order to look like you are really ignoring, you *must* be relaxed. Showing your child that you are annoyed (even if you don't say a word) won't work. You have to *show* no response. Think of Kenny Rogers's "The Gambler." You're at the table, your cards stink—but you 100 percent cannot let anyone else figure it out. It's the same situation here. I'll explain this more in step three. For now, just say "**I Li**ke **Re**laxed **Re**ading" a bunch of times. Write it down on the inside cover of this book and on the inside of the back cover. When you are sure you like relaxed reading, you are ready for step one.

Step One: Observe

In order for you to personalize this method for your family, you need to begin with a little bit of planning. You cannot ignore all undesirable behaviors. Some behaviors might be important to you. For example, table manners. If you want your children to simply stop goofing around at the dinner table, ignore them.

But if it is imperative for your children to have proper manners, using napkins and the correct spoon for soup, this might not be the best choice of behavior to ignore.

Before beginning to ignore behaviors, you have to know which ones are the most problematic. Is there anything your children do that really gets under your skin? For me, it is negotiating after I already said no to a request. My daughter asks for dessert, and I say, "Not today." She follows by asking ten more times, ten different ways (Nice daughter, pleading daughter, desperate daughter, angry daughter, oppressed daughter, etc.). She does this because she has learned that, in moments of weakness, this tactic can sometimes work.

For my friend Rory, it comes when her son looks her dead in the eyes and proceeds to throw a toy. He knows he shouldn't. I mean, he has heard the words, "We don't throw toys," at least one hundred times. And yet, he's thinking about it again. Both scenarios bring out an almost visceral reaction in Rory and me. The gravitational pull into that battle of wills is so strong that without proper preparation we would engage in the situation, thus reinforcing the undesirable behavior. These are our triggers, and our kids know it.

Now, here's a question to ask yourself: What are *your* triggers? What behaviors put you over the edge? What insanely annoying actions make you feel like jabbing pencils into your eyeballs? For some parents, this is easy. They can rattle off ten to fifteen actions that make them crazy. But for others, it just feels as if they are annoyed or frustrated all the time. They can't really pinpoint what's the worst of the behavior. It all feels sort of awful.

Even if you think you know where to start, do an exercise before beginning to ignore. Gaining insight into the parent-child dynamic and how it plays out will help you ignore much more effectively.

I want you to pretend to be a fly on the wall, following yourself around as you parent. What does that fly see? What did you reprimand? What made you raise your voice? Did you have to lecture anyone about proper behavior? What caused that lecture? What tactics did your kids employ to get your attention or push your buttons? Wait. Time-out. I know what you're thinking right now—yeah, I'm just going to move on to the next paragraph. Please don't. Analyzing your own parenting process is tremendously important if you want this to work. The process of Ignore it! isn't merely about your child. It's about you, too.

There is an observation form in Appendix C (I'll give you some examples below). Use it to monitor your behavior in response to your child and your child's behavior in response to you. Try to observe the dynamics until you have completed the page with at least ten interactions. For parents who are with their children for many hours during the day, or who find they discipline often, this will fill up quickly. For working parents or those who discipline a little less, this may take a few days. Stick with the process, because—again—it's an important step.

Some parents have a hard time observing themselves or acting naturally when they know they are being monitored (even if they are doing the monitoring). For these parents, I recommend setting an hourly alarm on your watch or cell phone. Every time you hear the alarm, write down what is going on at that moment. If there was anything notable during the last hour, write that down, too. Eventually, you will have your sheet filled out.

Here is an example of a completed observation form to help you understand how to fill it out.

Day	Time	Parent Feeling Rating Scale 1-10 1: Happy as a clam 10: Intensely frustrated, angry, or at breaking point	Precipitating Incident	Parent Reaction	Identify Trigger
Monday	8 a.m.	9	Trying to get Rachel to put shoes on for school. She is running around the house laughing in my face.	I kept calling her. I told her firmly to come right now. I gave consequences if she didn't come. Then I got mad and screamed at her. She came, but I felt horrible.	Rachel ignoring my request
Monday	12 p.m.	8	Rachel isn't eating her lunch. She is playing with it. Dropping it on the floor. She spilled milk on her pasta, too. I like to put her down for a nap by 12:30 so we can pick up her brother at school at 3 p.m. I am getting frustrated.	I keep telling her to hurry up and eat. Then I start begging. I explain also that I have to pick her brother up and she has to nap. She thinks this is a game and keeps at it.	Rachel pushing my buttons
Monday	4 p.m.	7-8	My son is singing a song he knows I don't like. And he is tapping his pencil nonstop while doing his homework.	I told him to stop singing and stop tapping his pencil. This went on for a long while. He had a smile on his face, and that made me angrier. Eventually, I lost it and moved him to the other room to finish his homework.	Singing and pencil tapping
Monday	7:30 p.m.	10	I'm exhausted. I want to get the kids in bed ASAP. Both kids are play-arguing and wrestling in the bathroom instead of getting ready for bed. They are laughing, and I hear them scheming to delay bedtime.	Yelling, threatening, more yelling. Every time I yell, they giggle. They know I am upset, and it is fun to them. This makes me feel defeated, and I grab their arms and yank them into bed.	Kids ganging up on me to change what is planned

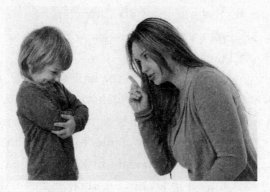

*This picture perfectly illustrates a child's reaction
when he gets a rise out of a parent. Mom's disciplining.
Son thinks it's funny.*

I added a rating scale to the chart because there is a correlation between how you are feeling and how you discipline. When you are relaxed and in a great mood, you almost certainly yell and discipline less frequently. Things that are borderline funny/annoying lean toward being more funny. A fart noise elicits a chuckle, not a lecture. When you are stressed, fed up, or angry, you become more attentive to annoying behaviors. The tapping of a pencil sounds like one thousand stampeding elephants. Agitated parents tend to discipline more often, but with less effectiveness.

The process of rating yourself is essential. Let's say you come home from work exhausted. Your jerk boss called you out about a mistake in front of your whole team. You splattered soup on your tie right before meeting an important client. The guy in the adjacent cubicle is hacking up a lung thanks to a bout with the latest flu. You overflowed the toilet in the men's room. Then you sat in traffic for forty-five minutes, which made you late to relieve the babysitter, which meant you had to pay her for an extra hour. By the time you walk through the door, you're less tolerant, and your coping skills have diminished (in other words, you're human).

When parents are pushed to the limits with life, they tend to fly off the handle more easily. Behavior that if they were less agitated wouldn't even register becomes a bigger issue. When this happens, parents either surrender to their children or they overcorrect, because every nudge, flick, and noise doubles as the most irksome act of all time. Yelling ensues and—at that moment—parenting becomes a job you'd gladly surrender in exchange for a soft bed in a dark room.

Make sure to complete your observation form before moving on to step two.

Step Two: Create a List of Target Behaviors

Now that you have completed your observation form, you should have more insight into your parenting dynamics. You surely can see what your children do that irritates you, and you should understand how you typically respond. In this step, you are going to focus simply on the triggers to create a list of target behaviors to ignore. This list isn't an end-all-be-all list. In other words, you don't have to ignore everything on the list. And conversely, you can ignore something that isn't on the list. Simply put, the point of the list is to help you make connections to the behavior so that when you see your children exhibiting that behavior you will know right away to ignore it instead of reacting.

Here are a few common triggers that may or may not be on your list:

- Kicking a parent's car seat
- Not sitting still at breakfast
- Dilly-dallying
- Talking loudly or yelling
- Nudging
- Messy eating, spilling, or dropping food from the table
- Complaining
- Mistreating books, throwing toys
- Play-fighting
- Baby talk
- Pencil chewing or tapping
- Nail-biting
- Whistling
- Using shirtsleeve as a napkin
- Whining
- Cursing
- Being disrespectful

Children do a lot to get their parents' attention, and attention-seeking is often behind trigger behaviors. Children yell and plead and stomp their feet. They tantrum and sometimes even hit. Why? Because they *want* a response. They want you to notice them. To look at them. To address them. And it usually works. Even if they don't get what they want (more time with their video game or another cookie), they get the second-best thing—your attention. That is usually reward enough for the behavior.

Here's an example: Jason is four, and a few months ago his parents brought home a baby brother named Tim. Before the little stinker came along, Jason was the sun in his parents' solar system. He was their everything. But along comes Tim. *Oh, isn't Tim cute! Isn't Tim wonderful! Look at Tim's smile! Tim! Tim! Tim!* Now Jason has to fight for his parents' affection, and he is not too jazzed about it. Making matters worse, that dreaded baby sure sucks up a ton of attention. He needs to be fed and changed—all the time. Jason is tired of competing. If he can't get his parents to play with him, Jason decides to act up until they have no choice but to deal. So what if he doesn't get snuggle time? At least he will get Mom and Dad away from that baby for a minute. His plan works like a charm, because whenever Jason throws a toy or climbs on something he shouldn't, his parents immediately shift their focus toward his direction.

This sort of pattern happens with only children, too. Take Winnie, for example. Generally, Winnie is a delight. Her parents enjoy bringing her out for dinner and on family outings. Winnie is used to getting a lot of attention. One day at the playground, Winnie couldn't wait to tell her mother she did a flip on the parallel bars. Mom, however, was busy talking to Winnie's teacher. Winnie knows she should wait and not interrupt, but she is too excited. She runs up to Mom and tries to interject. Mom quietly tells Winnie to wait a minute. Winnie retreats for eight seconds but grows restless. She begins to yank on Mom's shirt, tap her shoulder, whisper, "Mom, Mom, Mom." Eventually Mom turns to Winnie and shouts, "What is it?!" Presto! Winnie gets to tell her about the flip. Her mother may not be pleased at the moment, but it doesn't matter. Winnie stole her attention and was able to tell her the news. Mission accomplished.

There are many attention-seeking behaviors. Some are on that list already. But your child may have his own unique methodologies. Keep an eye out for those behaviors.

We have one more category of behaviors that should land on your list. These are behaviors that your child has a very difficult time controlling because of a condition or disability. For example, a child with ADHD may be very bouncy in his seat at the table or fidgety while doing his homework. A child with autism may make loud or repetitive noises. There is no benefit to disciplining what a child cannot control. Furthermore, your child may know that he doesn't have the ability to control these actions. Repetitively asking a child to stop these behaviors only makes him feel unaccepted and subpar. Ignoring this type of behavior also frees you up to work on what he can control.

Step Three: Ignore

You may be asking yourself, "How hard can it be to ignore my children?" Answer: extraordinarily hard. There is a gravitational pull that is involved in parent-child dynamics. When little people (and even big people) are pushing your buttons, going out of their way to exasperate you, and waiting for you to react, it can feel downright impossible not to surrender to the unhealthiest of impulses. That's the tricky part. But you can do it.

Here's how: you pretend. You pretend you don't care if your child is running around the house naked. You pretend it has no effect on you when your daughter dumps the toy chest in protest of a time-out. And you are only acting as if you don't mind one way or the other if your child refuses to eat the spaghetti she asked for three minutes ago. Deep down inside, you are probably upset, frustrated, fed up, angry, tired, at your wits' end, annoyed, etc. You want to throw a brick through the wall and smash the TV and squawk, "WHAT ARE YOU DO-ING????" (or something like that) as loud as you possibly can. But here's the thing: if your child sees any of that, you've lost the ball game. You're toast. He knows that his behavior is working on you, and he will just keep it up.

Ignoring is actually a skill. You have to learn it, because it doesn't come naturally. If you hear someone shouting in a restaurant, you turn your head. If someone is calling your name, you usually answer. And if someone at work taps you on the shoulder, you turn to say hello. It's a constructive, natural way to be. Overlooking things that are going on around us is not the norm.

The trick with selective ignoring is that you are not really ignoring your child. You are simply actively *not engaging*. You hear and see what is happening, but you will not react. This means you cannot make angry faces or stare with enlarged eyes or make any sounds. You won't threaten or provide consequences during this time. You will just go to a happy place in your mind and stay there for as long as it takes for the behavior to stop.

Sometimes, I tell parents to literally turn their back to the child. Walk away. You can even go to another room if that's safe and practical. You are trying to break the battle of wills and show your child that this behavior is ineffective. Feel free to pick up a catalog or magazine to flip through while you are disregarding your child's behavior. Take deep breaths. Sing the latest Taylor Swift song. Busy yourself getting the house cleaned up, packing your bag for work, or making dinner. Do not make eye contact. You can use your peripheral vision to keep track of your child's actions. Whatever you do, just make it clear that you are in no way reacting to your child.

Often when children see you not react, they think you didn't see or hear them. They may decide to ratchet up the behavior. This is normal, and we will review this phenomenon (called an "extinction burst") in Chapter 8. All I will say here is that this is where the resolve really comes in handy. You have decided to ignore these behaviors, and nothing your child will do or say will get you to engage in inappropriate behavior. Think of it as a game you *have to win*.

Tips for Ignoring Effectively

→ Do not make eye contact with the child.

→ Turn your back if you need help initiating Ignore it!.

→ Look busy doing something else.

→ Leave the room only if you can hear the child from the new location.

→ Do not show annoyance by nonverbal cues.

→ Do not make sounds that show your frustration.

Step Four: Listen

While you are actively ignoring your child's behavior, you are still listening and keeping track of his actions. This is a very important step. As I mentioned earlier, you are not really ignoring your child. You are just not engaging. We can't not engage forever, though. So we have to know when to reengage. This is why listening is imperative.

I want you to listen to your child carefully. As soon as your child stops the unacceptable behavior, then you can move on to step five. If you wait too long, your child will turn frustrated and engage in even more troubling behaviors. Ignoring isn't a punishment or a time-out. It is a method to improve behavior. That's the goal. So when you hear the child is no longer whining or complaining or throwing toys, start to reengage (step five).

If you are ignoring one of those behaviors that is difficult for your child to stop due to a condition or disability, this process is slightly different. The child may or may not finish doing the annoying or uncontrollable behavior. The goal here is for the parent to Ignore it! so that it doesn't impact the parent-child relationship. Over time, parents who ignore these behaviors suddenly realize they don't even notice them anymore. They learn to tune them out completely. The ignoring and listening steps give parents a little distance from annoying actions that cannot be stopped.

Step Five: Reengage

When parents are selectively ignoring, the goal is to improve behavior. Ignoring sends a nonverbal message that what the child is doing is not acceptable. (Again, the child who can't control the behavior isn't involved in the battle of wills and thus will not know you are even ignoring behavior.) Through this process, children learn that nagging, whining, and pushing buttons will have no impact on their parents. And when they learn that, we reengage.

Reengaging is when you enthusiastically begin to interact with your child again after the brief ignore period. You can—and should—talk and play and do any activities at this point. Some parents are still feeling frustrated or angry with their children after a difficult interaction. You must put that behind you, even if you have to fake it. If you are holding a grudge or not giving the child quality attention, you run the risk of your son or daughter acting out again.

Reengaging can be as simple as offering the child some Goldfish crackers or asking about her day at school. But it can also be playing LEGOs or Monopoly. A child who is begging to be noticed is letting the parent know (sometimes in inappropriate ways) he needs some attention. Ignoring the begging doesn't negate the fact that the child is reaching out for attention. Ignore it! teaches children that inappropriate behavior will not work when it comes to scoring attention or a material item. However, parents can't ignore the underlying need that is being presented. When the undesirable or inappropriate behavior stops, immediately get back in there with all of the happiness of a fresh-baked slice of homemade apple pie (à la mode, with whipped cream). If you don't feel it, remember to fake it.

I've done this a million times. Some days it's easy. Maybe I never got that worked up during the exchange. And some days it takes all my strength. No matter what, the quickest way to help children move on is for the parent to move on, too. During the reengagement phase, make sure not to discuss the previous incident, because that is not moving on. Don't say, "Honey, I was ignoring you because . . ." It will just rehash the problem and provide the attention/benefit you were trying to avoid. Also, it's much more effective to have a conversation in advance about expectations for behavior. I'll talk more about setting up clear expectations in Chapter 10.

Oh, and if you try to reengage and the child is still having a meltdown or begins the annoying behavior again, go back to step three and Ignore it!.

Step Six: Repair

Sometimes when children are acting out or throwing a tantrum, they might cause hurt to someone or destroy some property. This, too, can happen during Ignore it!. Maybe an aggravated little Joanna threw a box of crayons across the floor or Jimmy Jr. hit his mother on the leg when Ignore it! incensed him. If a behavior takes place that calls for the child to make amends, do that in step six.

This step is optional. It only is necessary to take care of any hurt feelings, battered property, or issues that arose during the ignoring step. This includes apologizing for hurting someone and cleaning up toys or objects that were thrown in a tantrum.

Additionally, there may be something for which the parent needs to apologize. If you dropped some excessively harsh words, say you're sorry. Showing your child that you made a mistake—and you are willing to take responsibility for it—is *incredibly* important. It also helps to move on from whatever issue you were ignoring.

Ignore it! isn't easy. Actually, it is unequivocally hard. Kids are masters at getting our attention. It takes practice and inner strength to step back and not engage in the inappropriate conduct. But as we discussed in earlier chapters, the benefits are massive. You will minimize attention-seeking or annoying behavior. You will enjoy your parenting time more, and you and your children will actually feel better. So this process is more than worth the effort.

Ignore it! may feel strange or unnatural at first. To some, it is a thoroughly counterintuitive idea to ignore children when they are acting out. It might take a while for the concepts to feel right to you. If you are still feeling unsure, the next few chapters will help. I'll provide many examples of Ignore it! in action to exhibit how it works in reality. Through the scenarios, all of the concepts will become even clearer.

Important Points to Remember

- **I Like Re**laxed **Re**ading: Ignore, Listen, Reengage, and Repair.
- There is a correlation between how you are feeling and how you discipline.
- There is no benefit to disciplining what a child cannot control.
- Ignore it! is extraordinarily hard, and it takes conscientiousness and practice to perfect.
- When you are ignoring, you are actively not engaging.
- Listening while ignoring is imperative to know when to stop ignoring and reengage.
- Don't make eye contact while in the ignoring step.
- When reengaging, be enthusiastic even if you have to fake it.

CHAPTER 5

Sample Scenarios

THE DEVIL IS in the details. That's an old saying that means sometimes when something seems so simple there is a hidden complication that can derail success. Have you ever been lost? I can't imagine that anyone hasn't been lost at least once. Well, sometimes directions seem fairly straightforward. But somehow, if you make one left when you should have made a right, you get completely lost. One minor mistake can have a tremendous impact.

Once, when she was in high school, my older sister, Leah, set out to make these Greek butter cookies. She had all the ingredients meticulously lined up on the counter. Then—the screwup. Instead of using baking powder, she accidentally poured in baking soda. What emerged from the oven were oblong hockey pucks, as edible as slabs of rubberized tire. They were quickly disposed of. But that's the thing—that one small misstep completely undermined an entire effort. It happens with baking. And it 100 percent happens with parenting. With Ignore it!, it's somewhat easy to mess up by overlooking a step in the process or by getting befuddled by a nuance. Hence, in this chapter I hope to minimize potential derailments by giving you loads of samples of Ignore it! in action.

On a side note, my sister's baking powder/soda mix-up has left a permanent impression on me. I'm completely paranoid about using the wrong powder. I obsessively check the recipe and then the container several times to make sure to use the correct one. I bake often and have never made that mistake. Why? Because messing up can be instructive. With Ignore it!, it is no big deal if you respond when you shouldn't have. You just need to start over the next time. Sure, you might have undone the progress you were making. But if you made progress once, you can make it again. And the second time is much more likely to stick because you will be more aware of your mistake . . . like I am in baking.

Just to review, please keep in mind "I Like Relaxed Reading." It stands for the four main steps to the Ignore it! process: Ignore, Listen, Reengage, and Repair. While reading the situations in the rest of the chapter, try to make note of each stage. This will help you become an expert in the technique and will really help you in the moment when you implement Ignore it!.

Negotiating

A mother called me just last week to get some help with Eleanor, her strong-willed five-year-old daughter. Mom told me her child negotiates about absolutely everything. So I asked Mom what usually happens when Eleanor negotiates. "Well, I don't give in to her demands," she replied. "Usually, we meet somewhere in the middle, so it feels like we both win." Um, no. You aren't winning. As soon as I explained why Eleanor negotiates (because the tactic works), Mom had her lightbulb moment. She realized that any negotiation was a win for Eleanor and it just made her do it more. And more. And more. I told Eleanor's mother to make decisions on some of the nonnegotiable rules in her house and to start enforcing them without discussion. For example, Mom wanted Eleanor to sit at the table for meals instead of on the couch. Eleanor likes to watch television while she eats. Eleanor's mom really didn't want to allow it, but it seemed to be the only way Eleanor would consume food. Mom decided that from now on Eleanor would not be allowed to eat on the couch.

The next day at lunchtime, Eleanor went to the couch and sat down in her usual spot. Her mom entered the room (a little parenting tip: never yell requests from another room) and told Eleanor lunch was ready on the table. Eleanor was befuddled and went right into mediation mode.

"Why can't I eat by the television?"

"But I always eat on the couch."

"Can't I just watch and eat this one last time?" (Mom almost fell for this one.)

"How about I eat on the couch but then I'll come to the table to drink my milk?"

"What if I eat at the table but you move it to be in front of the TV?"

As Eleanor tried to negotiate, Mom made her own lunch, very slowly making a sandwich for herself. She worked on the food slowly, deliberately, because she feared if she looked at Eleanor she would crack and give in. Eleanor turned angry. Mom kept her resolve. Eleanor started to shout that she wouldn't eat.

Mom stayed the course, keeping lunch on the table. Eleanor got mean and insulted Mom, but Mom just ignored every outburst. Mom took her sandwich to the table and choked down a few bites while flipping through a catalog (as I told her to do). She didn't move Eleanor's lunch. She didn't make eye contact, and she didn't engage. Every time Eleanor would try to kick-start the negotiation, Mom acted as if she didn't hear it.

Mom was carefully keeping an eye on Eleanor, who—in the name of dramatic impact—was lying across the doorway between the kitchen and the family room. But ultimately, pride gave in to hunger and reality. Eleanor wanted to eat. She saw Mom wasn't cracking. Suddenly, she rose, walked to the table, sat down, and ate. Inside, Mom was both euphoric and shocked. She had been dreading this task the entire day. Now, flying high, Mom closed her catalog and excitedly began to discuss a dear friend's visit for that afternoon. The focus was off of where lunch was being eaten. After a few minutes of conversation, Mom told Eleanor that she was doing a great job eating her sandwich.

Eleanor's mom told me her daughter hadn't eaten anything at the table in eons. She'd thought it wasn't possible. If she had known that all she would have had to do to get Eleanor back to the table was to ignore her negotiating and outbursts, she would have done it years earlier. She said it would have saved hours and hours of arguments.

Bedtime

Addie is an eleven-year-old only child who is very close to her divorced mother. Addie's mom absolutely adores Addie. She works considerably long hours, but likes to give Addie all of her attention when she can. However, Addie's mom has consistently dealt with one issue every single day since Addie was a baby. Namely, Addie possesses an arsenal filled with techniques to keep from going to bed.

When Mom arrives home from work, she has a hard time saying no to Addie—and the child knows it. So when it comes time for bed, Addie turns on the charm. She asks Mom to tell her stories from childhood. She tries to snuggle just a little bit longer. The list of people in Addie's prayers lengthens more every day. It started with her parents. Then her aunts and uncles and grandparents. Now she's praying for the guy at the grocery store, the New York Mets, Taylor Swift, the person who invented scissors, and the mail lady. She needs a sip of water. Her toe hurts. She forgot to have a paper for school signed. She's nervous for a test. Could she just quickly grab a bite to eat because she is still hungry? Oh, wait. Now her stomach hurts. She forgot to plug in her cell phone. There is a strange sound outside her window. And so it goes. Every. Single. Night.

Fed up with this ordeal, Mom contacted me to help resolve this problem. She wanted Addie to say her prayers, have a quick tuck-in, and just go to sleep. When I asked Mom how she handles Addie when she prolongs bedtime, she sighed and then gave me a laundry list of lame responses ranging from "Okay, honey, go to sleep" to "You better get your butt in that bed and stay there!" Sometimes Mom felt Addie really needed something, so she provided the water, a warmer blanket, or Addie's retainers (Mom had already spent $3,000 on orthodontia and she wasn't about to let those teeth go to pot just because Addie can't remember to put those darn retainers in at night). It was clear that Addie had cracked her mom's code. Mom couldn't resist responding to Addie. She loved her dearly, after all. It would be rude not to respond to her requests.

I explained to Mom that Addie knows she is loved, and ignoring some of these nightly extravagances wouldn't shake that bond. Addie wasn't carrying on because she felt slighted or unloved. No, she was behaving as such because she could. Addie called out and Mom responded, and the entire ritual encouraged the child to call out again and again.

After our chat, however, Mom was catching on to the pattern and learning how to Ignore it!. The very next evening, Mom told Addie that after she said good night she would not engage in any additional conversation until morning. I told Mom that if for some reason Addie woke up in the middle of the night and seemed sick, she should, of course, check on her.

Addie didn't really take Mom seriously because she has always been able to manipulate her. So Addie got in bed, said her prayers, and then Mom said good night and left the room. Immediately, Addie started to call out. The calls got louder and angrier each time. Eventually, Addie rose from her bed and found Mom, who was putting away the laundry. The daughter cleared her throat and said, loudly, "Mom, seriously, I needed to tell you something!"

Mom was beside herself trying not to ask Addie what she had to tell her. Again, in Mom's head, she is thinking it is rude not to answer her daughter. But then she remembered that I told her that Addie would probably get very creative and sneaky trying to get her mom to engage.

Addie carries on: "Mom, are you listening? I have to tell you something really important that happened at school." This is a soft spot for Mom. She prides herself on being available for

Addie and knowing all that is going on in her life. Sensing that she is getting too close for comfort, Mom heads into her bathroom and begins brushing her teeth. Addie yells, "Oh. My. Gosh. Are you ignoring me? Fine. I *won't* tell you what happened." She turns and leaves the room. Mom takes a deep breath. Was it really going to be that easy?

Nope. Addie is back. "Mom, I have a stomachache." Now this would normally throw Mom into a tizzy. If Addie is sick tomorrow, that would throw off her work plans, and she has a major meeting at eight a.m. But this time Mom doesn't react at all. Addie wasn't sick two minutes ago. Mom starts to see it so clearly now. All this time she was encouraging Addie's behavior. Of course she resisted bedtime—because Mom let her. Now Mom was resolved. She was going to win this war once and for all.

Addie tested Mom for more than an hour. It escalated. Addie got furious. She cried and whimpered on and off. This was really hard for Mom. But eventually, Addie went to bed. Mom was afraid of encountering Addie in the morning. She was sure Addie would give her the cold shoulder. I had instructed Mom to engage Addie in a very joyful, positive manner and start chatting as soon as she saw her. Mom did and Addie never mentioned the night before.

The following evening, Mom once again told Addie that after she said good night she wouldn't return. Addie should put herself to sleep. Now Mom introduced a reward for Addie.

She told her that if she stayed in her room all night she could buy a new song on iTunes in the morning before school (I'll discuss more about rewards in Chapter 9). Addie was fanatical about music. This worked like a charm. Addie did call out a bunch of times, but she never left her room, and she was asleep in about thirty minutes. Mom continued the reward system as well as Ignore it! every night that week, and by the weekend Addie no longer resisted bedtime. It turned out she enjoyed reading a little on her own and putting herself to sleep. And she loved getting new songs every day. Eventually, when Addie stopped calling out at bedtime and never left her room for several weeks, Mom told Addie that she was so proud of her accomplishment. Mom didn't want to reward her forever for this behavior. We discussed finding a big surprise for Addie to celebrate. Mom located a concert in the area that Addie would love. They went together and Mom gushed about her pride in how Addie had changed. But really it was Mom who had changed. Mom continued to show Addie her pleasure at the new bedtime routine because it was important for Addie to still get the attention she needed. However, after the concert Mom discontinued any material rewards for bedtime behavior.

Dinner

Mealtime at Steve and Dottie Johnson's house is a nightmare. Their preschooler son Jack is becoming a very picky eater. When his mom asks if he wants pasta or grilled cheese for lunch, he says, "Pasta." But when Dottie brings Jack his pasta, he immediately says, "I didn't want pasta. I'm not going to eat it." Before reading Ignore it!, Dottie would try to rationalize with Jack. She'd explain that he had indeed asked for the pasta. "It is the same pasta you loved last night for dinner," she'd say. Continuing to sell the pasta, she'd say, "You need to eat to grow up to be tall like daddy." Every effort to get Jack to eat just made him more resolute. He'd emphatically declare, "I will not eat it—ever!" Jack knew instinctively that his mother cared a great deal about his nutrition because he was small for his age and very thin. He actually loves pasta but enjoys seeing his mother rush about the kitchen even more.

After applying Ignore it!, meals are a whole lot more enjoyable. Dottie still asks Jack what he would like and then she gives it to him. But as soon as the complaining begins, she turns away from Jack. Sometimes she gets up to pretend to busy herself at the stove. Other times, she grabs herself a drink. But she doesn't engage with Jack if he is complaining about the meal. She decides that if he doesn't want to eat what *he* asked for, then he will just have to be a little hungry until the next meal. But a funny thing happens when Dottie ignores Jack. The battle of wills never begins. Jack notices his mom isn't begging him to eat like she usually does. And she isn't even offering to make him something else. Feeling hungry, Jack decides on his own to start eating. Dottie is overcome with glee, but she doesn't show it. As soon as she sees Jack is eating his food, she begins to reengage him by asking what he would like to do after his nap.

Dinner 2

If left to her own devices, my daughter would eat only bread, pasta, cheese, and sweets, with an occasional bowl of cereal with milk. We have come to an unspoken agreement that I would prepare her food plain but I would expect her to eat what the rest of the family was eating. For example, when I make tacos, I take out some of the browned meat for her before adding in the seasoning. If I am making hamburgers, she likes hers with only salt, so I accommodate. I will not be a short-order cook and make a different meal for everyone. But I do feel she has simple tastes, and within reason I can try to prepare her food to match her preferences.

Most days she takes a look at the food and says, "Oh no, not [fill in the blank with pretty much any food that exists on the planet we call Earth]." She starts with complaining and trying to negotiate another option.

TODAY:

> *Casey: What's for dinner?*
> *Me: Steak and a potato.*
> *Casey: I don't like potatoes. Can I have my steak on a roll?*
> *Me: No. You can have just steak, then.*
> *Casey: Please? Why can't I have bread instead of potato? Mom!*
> *Me:* [Not a word. I'm ignoring her.]
> *Casey: Can I have the leftover rice?*
> *Me:* [I'm in my happy place. I will not engage. I will not engage.]
> *Casey (after a short internal deliberation): I'll have a potato.*

Some days, my daughter decides she is too hungry to pass up what is being offered. Other days, she eats only a small amount of dinner. No snacks are offered after dinner and no substitutions are made once dinner is on the table. Even though she still likes to show her displeasure, it doesn't turn into an argument or full-blown negotiation. She knows that once I answer her initial request I will not discuss it again.

Winter Coat

If you live in any state north of the Mason-Dixon line you are familiar with the winter coat phenomenon. This is when, quite suddenly, boys (and sometimes girls) simply stop wanting to wear a coat, even in the dead of winter. It's possible the need to fit in and look good at all times is the driving force. Or maybe teens—overcome by raging hormones—simply don't feel the cold as normal humanoids do. Whatever the case, this is a consistent battle in thousands upon thousands of American homes. Child wants to go to school sans jacket, and parents insist one must be worn.

This is the case with Jackie and her fifteen-year-old son, Liam. Jackie tries to allow Liam some flexibility. He can keep his room messy. He doesn't have an assigned bedtime during the weekends. But she goes absolutely berserk when Liam won't wear his coat. She feels it makes her look like an irresponsible parent when he walks all over the neighborhood without it, and she worries he will get sick. In an effort to resolve this issue, Jackie instituted a rule that if the weather forecast called for a temperature below forty-five degrees, Liam would take his jacket to school. The boy begrudgingly agreed.

Of course it wasn't that simple. One day the temperature was slated to be a high of forty-five. However, the high would not be reached until four p.m., after the school day ended. Jackie insisted Liam take his coat. Jackie and Liam are known to enter the battle of wills and their battles often end in escalating tension. Generally, Jackie tries to explain to Liam why she is right about something. Liam argues, and when he doesn't get his way he punches the wall or throws an item across the room.

On this occasion, the discussion starts as usual. Liam pleads nicely. Jackie explains her point of view and demands Liam take his coat. Liam argues some more, and ultimately Jackie says, "Liam, I'm done discussing this. You are wearing your jacket." Now Liam turns mean. He senses that his mom is near her breaking point. He insults his mother by telling her that she is ugly, fat, and stupid.

Jackie tries to walk away. Liam continues his rant until Jackie can't take it anymore. She starts to scream at Liam. Back and forth they go, each trying to outscream the other. Even Jackie gets a little mean. She has no time for this before work. Eventually, Jackie gives up. She says, "Wear what you want. Catch pneumonia or freeze to death. I don't give a crap."

Liam and Jackie both silently leave the room. Both feel bad about how the situation went down. But the bottom line is that Liam doesn't have to wear his coat. All of that carrying on and name-calling works to get his mom to give up. After each one of these interactions a small chip of their relationship is sacrificed. Jackie worries about how these battles push her son further away from her.

I reviewed the situation with Jackie. She admits that in general she should ignore much of Liam's angry outbursts. I told her that Liam goes for the jugular because he has learned that hurting her feelings is an effective way to get what he wants or to get out of doing something. In this case, his behavior was negatively reinforced because the jacket requirement was removed. Even though Liam always feels remorse after these exchanges, you can bet he will continue to walk the same path because it is highly effective.

Jackie and I discussed picking battles with Liam. The coat

fight wasn't worth the effort. Jackie cannot make Liam wear the coat once he leaves the house. It's guaranteed that before he even reaches the bus stop his coat is stuffed into his backpack. Mom should let natural consequences take over (more on natural consequences in Chapter 10). If one day Liam gets cold, next time he will bring his coat. Once he is off at college, she won't be able to mandate his clothing. Jackie understood this logic. And she understood clearly that she cannot resolve a disagreement by arguing with Liam. From now on, if she sees Liam getting frustrated and angry about a decision she makes, she will ignore all negotiation, mean comments, or any strategy Liam employs to get her to engage in an argument and potentially change her mind. Jackie will be much more careful about what she imposes on Liam, but if she states a requirement she must stick to it.

Liam is an angry child and his relationship with his mother is complex. Although he can display affection toward Jackie, he is often distant and aloof. Jackie has a very strained relationship with her parents and is concerned that she is setting up the same pattern with Liam. Jackie has learned through Ignore it! that each interaction with Liam ending in a screaming match only reinforces his behavior, moving her further from her stated goal. This will not be resolved quickly. However, Jackie can minimize the damage done (emotionally and physically) by ignoring Liam's inappropriate outbursts.

Cursing and Back Talk

Parents often call me because their child has taken to saying "Shit" or "Goddamn it!" after a parent accidentally let it slip.

This happened to me one day. I took my two kids to the doctor because my daughter had a high fever. I parked next to a giant cement pillar. As I parked I thought to myself, *Be careful getting out of here.* But by the time we got back in the car I was in a rush and completely forgot about the pillar. As I pulled out, guess what happened? Yup, I smacked into the pillar and screamed, "Shit!"

Now, I almost never curse, and my husband can back me up on this. But in that moment of pure fury I let it slip. And my children were listening intently. The inevitable happened shortly thereafter, and "shit" became a household word for a hot minute.

When something like this happens, and children learn an inappropriate word, parents usually respond with a bold "Don't say that!" The child may have no idea what he is saying, but he knows enough that it produces an instant response and attention. Here's the funny thing: when I tell parents to just Ignore it!, I'm almost always greeted with that sideways look and something along the lines of, "No way—if I ignore it my kids will think that sort of language is okay." But, well, they're wrong. Yes, the child will probably continue saying the bad words for a short time. But it will end quickly, because the whole point is inspiring the reaction—only there is none.

Unlike the inadvertent cursing I just discussed, some kids use extremely disrespectful language directed toward their parents. I've seen seven-year-olds with tongues as filthy as a public bathroom floor at the beach. Teenagers also can mix attitude with hurtful words in a way that cuts to the core of any mother or father. Most parents have a low threshold for back talk. When children spew anger, their parents feel disrespected and embarrassed, and they almost always respond to the disrespect with a "You can't talk to me like that!" There is a fundamental problem with this approach. It is physically impossible to prevent a child from saying something. Children *can* talk to parents like that. And when parents get angry, children feel successful in having done something hurtful to the parent. If a child feels anger, sometimes he wants a parent to feel anger, too.

Jennifer is the mom of thirteen-year-old Justin. Jennifer had Justin when she was just a teenager herself. For a long time, she had a drug problem, but has been in recovery and clean for eight years. Although he doesn't express it well, Justin harbors a good deal of resentment toward his mother due to some of what he missed in the early days. Jennifer told me that whenever Justin doesn't get what he wants, he goes for the jugular. For example, Jennifer told him that he couldn't go out with friends until he cleaned his room. Justin was angry and lashed out with "I hate you! I am going to start doing drugs soon! I can't take this life!" Even though Jennifer knows he is just saying that to get to her, it really breaks her heart. Of all the misery in the world, what she fears most is Justin following her path into drug abuse. Mom and son are in a therapy program to help with some of the psychological damage that both are experiencing. However, Jennifer is also using Ignore it! to stop reacting to Justin's outbursts.

Intellectually, she knows Justin doesn't mean his words. Ignoring it is the quickest way to get Justin to stop expressing his anger to spite his mother. Now, when Justin says he will do drugs in a moment of passion, she completely ignores him. As soon as Justin calms down, she engages him by validating his anger. Jennifer says, "I can see that you are really angry."

Instead of discussing potential drug use, Jennifer focuses on the immediate issue that evoked her son's anger.

The technique has worked beautifully, and Justin has stopped threatening to use drugs as a way to hurt or anger Jennifer. He still turns frustrated but is able to calm down and discuss what is bothering him instead of deflecting. Mom is better at dealing with Justin's frustration, too, because she is working on her own guilt about her past drug use.

Drama Queen

Randi is a drama queen. She has an overblown reaction to everything. She gets hysterical with the slightest bump or bruise. She tantrums extensively when she doesn't get her way. And she will do just about anything to snag attention. Her parents have mostly laughed off her overindulgences with the ol' "It's just Randi being Randi." However, now that Randi is seven, her outbursts aren't as cute as they once were. It feels as if Randi is in a constant battle with her little brother for her parents' attention.

Randi's parents applied Ignore it! to Randi's behavior whenever she was trying to get a reaction or acting inappropriately. Randi's parents thought about what kind of behaviors they were looking for. I explained that they should keep an eye out for overblown responses, negotiating, and crying without tears.

One day at a birthday party, Randi wanted to have a second cupcake. After her request was denied, she turned hysterical in front of everyone at the party. It was humiliating times one thousand, and it wasn't easy for Randi's parents to look the other way. But they did, because they knew this was a test.

Randi kept looking over at her mom and dad to see if anything she was trying was working. And while Randi's parents were turned away, they, too, were watching Randi. As soon as Randi calmed down and stopped carrying on, her parents engaged. They asked her if she wanted to play a few games before leaving the party. Randi regrouped without having a second cupcake and moved on. Randi's parents also learned to praise Randi repeatedly when she got it right the first time. If she was disappointed in something but she kept it together, her parents would say how proud they were of her. If she didn't get her way but didn't throw a tantrum, she was rewarded with excessive attention. Her parents might rave, "Wow, Randi, you have a great attitude!" or "Look how well you handled your disappointment. We are so proud of you." Over time, Randi learned that her tantrums had no effect on her parents and they mostly disappeared. Randi still leaned toward the dramatic, but her behavior was no longer inappropriate or draining to her parents.

CHAPTER 6

Time-Out

I F THERE HAS ever been a more misunderstood or misused parenting technique than the ubiquitous time-out, well, I haven't seen it. Time-out is an excellent behavior improvement method for the parenting toolbox, and it meshes perfectly with Ignore it!.

However, the majority of people I've worked with are lost when it comes to the implementation of time-out. What should be a very brief break turns into an excruciating battle of wills. Just like the behavior modification principles I discussed in Chapter 2, the effectiveness of time-out is well researched. It has been found to be highly successful in reducing talking back, noncooperation, oppositionality, destruction of property, yelling, nagging, hitting, and biting. It's also effective with children who have been diagnosed with a variety of developmental disorders. But the time-out only truly works when it is executed properly.

The Internet offers loads of faulty or inaccurate information about time-out. Conscientious parents are making mistakes with the best of intentions. Unfortunately, the end result is often an increase in unwanted behavior and confused, frustrated mothers and fathers who, at wits' end, ultimately drop the technique.

Remember my friend Rory from Chapter 4? She's the one who goes crazy when her son not only ignores her directives, but deliberately continues with the bad behavior. Her three-year-old son, Johnny, is a smart cookie. He knows exactly what to do to draw Mom's attention, and not in a good way. He throws a toy. She says, "Johnny, we don't throw toys." Johnny is thinking, *Well, actually, we do,* and then launches his mini-piano across the room. As the sound of one hundred scattered plastic pieces rises from the floor, Rory storms toward her smug offspring, picks him up, and puts him in his time-out chair.

"You are in time-out!" she says sternly. "Stay here until I tell you to get out!"

Not only is Johnny unmoved, he actually chips away at Rory's resolve. First, he gets up, shuffles a foot from the chair, and says, in the "to hell with you" voice that Rory loathes, "I'm not in my chair." Rory goes right back and plants him back in the chair. He gets up again, and she yells, "You better get back in that chair." Johnny sits. But the chatter starts. Johnny transitions to the sweet phase, knowing what's worked in the past.

"Mommy, can I get up now?"
"Mommy, can I have peanut butter for lunch?"
"Mommy, will you read me *Bedtime Bunny* before nap?"
"Mommy, you make the best chocolate cupcakes."

As her son jabbers away, Rory takes care of a few things around the house. Johnny sits quietly. But then he gets bored and mischievous. He starts yanking at the curtains behind the couch next to where he is seated. Soon the ruffles start unraveling. *Oh, this is cool*, he thinks.

He pulls apart a large section of the curtains. Suddenly Rory realizes that it's too quiet. She runs in to see the mess Johnny made, and she is beyond furious. She tells him to just leave her alone. Johnny runs off into his room. He isn't quite sure what happened, but he can tell his mom is mad. He's just happy to be out of time-out. When Rory is done cleaning up the mess, she gets Johnny and orders him to put his mini-piano away. He knows he is in a bit of trouble now, so he complies. This is a dysfunctional time-out. I'll explain why shortly.

A stay-at-home dad I know had a similar experience. His son Jayden is a bit of a troublemaker. Nice boy, but naughty. Dad often puts him in time-out. Because Jayden is six, Dad puts him in time-out for six minutes. But it is never merely six minutes—because Jayden can't sit on the darn step for that long. Every time Jayden gets up, Dad resets the timer. And with each reset comes arguing, negotiation, and a large expanse of wasted time. Instead of the time-out being a momentary separation, it is an intense battle of wills. The average time-out lasts a good thirty minutes longer than intended. Jayden's dad tells me he is ready to give up on time-outs. He thinks the technique won't work for his son.

Both Rory and Jayden's father commit classic mistakes that result in time-outs turning into—at best—exercises in frustration and—at worst—ineffective time drains. Adding to the agony is that with every time-out, both parents are reinforcing Johnny's and Jayden's bad behavior. Every time the child violates the basic conditions of the time-out, the reward is extra attention. It's the absolute worst end result. When a child gets the benefit of attention for undesirable behavior, they are prone to repeat it. The most upsetting outcome though is that both Rory and Jayden's dad are giving up on time-out. That is the ultimate win for the kids. One less disciplinary technique being used means more free rein.

Before I show you how Ignore it! completely changes the time-out game, I want to clarify what time-out is *not*. Having a firm understanding of time-out will help you avoid some of the ways parents get off track.

Time-Out Is Not a Punishment

Time-out is not a punishment, and that's important enough for me to say twice. *Time-out is not a punishment.*

Parents often complain that they use time-outs to punish the child for bad behavior, but they can't get the child to stay in time-out. So a five-minute time-out becomes a twenty-minute circus. Instead of a punishment, think of time-out as a restart button. The main purpose of giving a child a time-out is to break the behavior pattern and allow the child to move on to more appropriate behavior. Time-out is also a good way for both parent and child to emotionally calm down and break the battle of wills. If time-out is conducted properly, there is no communication between parent and child, thereby allowing for the needed break. I'm not saying parents should give kids a time-out in order to get a few minutes to calm down. There are better ways to disengage using Ignore it!. But, if done correctly, it is a side benefit.

Time-Out Should Not Be Timed by Age

I don't know who first promoted the idea that children should sit in time-out one minute for each year of age, but it is a rotten idea. Giving children too much time in time-out only provides them with opportunity to resume problematic behavior. Some children understand right away what they did wrong, and they are ready to change their ways. But sitting for several more minutes only pushes that acknowledgment further from their minds and allows new ideas to enter the cranium.

During many home visit observations, I have seen time-outs that should have ended but didn't. When the child feels as if the time-out will never end, he gets restless and, often, mischievous. There is no evidence that longer time-outs are more effective. However, some evidence shows that time-outs lasting one to two minutes might be too easy an out. So if you need a rule of thumb, aim for a long enough break where the child really feels the loss of attention and reinforcement but not too long where the child gets into trouble. Somewhere around two to three minutes is just right.

Time-Out Doesn't Need a Specific Location

Many people have a time-out spot. There is nothing necessarily wrong with this practice. However, it eliminates the ability to have time-out outside the house. And if the child doesn't stay in the designated location, the parent endlessly tries to enforce sitting in the spot. This removes focus from the purpose of the time-out and interrupts the process. Think of time-out as removing attention rather than setting the child in a specific spot. Using Ignore it! allows time-outs to be given anywhere, anytime.

Time-Out Isn't a Banishment

When children don't remain in their assigned spot for the time-out, parents generally become frustrated and often enraged. How will they be able to give the time-out if they can't physically keep the child in the time-out place? So parents frequently decide to move the time-out location to the child's bedroom, and shut the door behind the child. Now the parent has to stand outside the door, holding it shut until Junior does the allotted time-out.

This is so wrong for several reasons. A child's room should be a sacred, joyous place where a boy or girl feels loved and safe. If the bedroom isn't respected in that way, then the child could cease wanting to be there. The child could become scared with the door shut. We should never do anything that might frighten our kids. There are long-term consequences to this, and it's damage that can't be seen. Before you know it, the child might soon have trouble falling asleep and end up in your bed at night. Alternatively, you might have to sit by the bed for an hour while the child dozes off.

In a time-out where the door is closed, parents have no idea what is going on behind it. For all the parent knows, the child may be happily playing with his toys while he is in time-out.

That deflects from the purpose. Also, if the door is closed, it is possible the child is unsafe and unsupervised. Let's say the child is in time-out and you hear a loud thump. Do you open the door? Is time-out over? How would a parent not open the door? I imagine the door opens and the parent either sees a child buried under a dresser that wasn't secured during a tantrum or the parent sees a smiling, petulant child who knows he won the game. If a boy or girl in time-out finds a way to get attention, you can be sure to expect that same behavior in the future.

Sometimes, children locked in their rooms try to escape by yanking constantly at the door. Having a tug-of-war with the door handle isn't exactly disengaging. It's precisely the opposite. A parent must be giving continual attention in order to keep the door closed. This goes against the principles of time-out.

So What *Is* Time-Out?

Time-out is Ignore it! in action. In Ignore it!, we remove attention and the benefits of our attention to send a message that a behavior is inappropriate. Time-out is exactly the same. It's detaching the child from any kind of reinforcement. Remember from Chapter 2 that reinforcement is defined as any action that makes a behavior more likely to occur. In other words, any behavior that is reinforced will be repeated. And attention is reinforcement. Time-out, when done correctly, removes attention and thus any reinforcement. Consequently, unwanted behavior generally diminishes.

Basically, time-out is just a short period of ignoring to withdraw attention. If the benefits of pushing a parent's buttons are removed, there is no incentive to act up. The process teaches a child that pushing, throwing toys, nagging, harassing, spitting, and other undesirable behaviors are not acceptable and no attention will reinforce those activities. Also, children don't want to be removed from their play area or from the family environment. Being removed completely takes the fun out of being bad. That is the purpose of a time-out: just to remove attention. That's it. So in a time-out, just as in Ignore it!, when the behavior stops we immediately reengage the child.

Steps for Time-Out with Ignore It!

Using Ignore it! in time-out helps parents focus on the purpose and not interfere with the process. Here are the steps to follow for an effective time-out:

- If you see inappropriate behavior, give no more than one warning that if the behavior continues there will be a time-out. If the behavior involves hitting or something egregious (like biting), put the kid into time-out without a warning.
- Immediately following the undesirable behavior, declare, "You are in time-out for [fill in the behavior]. Go to [a place away from you for the time-out]."
- If the child is younger than six, take him by the hand and walk him to the location.
- Just before walking away, say, "You are in time-out until you calm down and are ready to [apologize, clean up, stop doing whatever sent child to time-out]."
- Now tell yourself "**I Like Re**laxed **Re**ading."

- Begin Ignore it! by disregarding any attention-seeking behavior.
- Listen carefully. As soon as the child is calm and quiet, go back and end the time-out.
- Reengage the child by very briefly reminding him why you put him in time-out.
- Repair as needed by having the child apologize and/or clean up. This is an important step because the time-out isn't an escape from doing what is required. If the child is excused after the time-out without doing the repair, it is possible the behavior that put the child in the time-out will be reinforced. For example, child throws toys all around the room. Dad puts child in time-out. After time-out, it is dinnertime and Dad decides to clean up toys himself after bedtime. Now the child knows exactly what to do to get out of cleaning up before dinner.
- Move on after the time-out, as if the behavior never happened. You might still be frustrated or angry. Suppress all signs of it and act positively toward your child. Quickly try to praise child for any appropriate behavior exhibited.

Here is how time-out should work with Ignore it!:

Jessica and her little sister Kate are wrapping up lunch. Mom promised the girls they could have some cookies after they finished their sandwiches. She puts a bowl of mini–chocolate chip cookies in front of each girl. Jessica gobbles hers down in three minutes flat. Kate takes her time with each cookie. She likes to look at them carefully to save the best one for last. Then she nibbles each one slowly.

When Mom turns to wash the dishes, Jessica tries to steal a cookie from Kate. Kate begins to scream. Mom isn't happy. "Jessica," she bellows, "if you touch her bowl again, you will go to time-out!" Now Mom turns away to give Jessica a chance to change her behavior without feeling the need to test her mom.

Jessica is just too tempted, so she steals a cookie. Mom sees this from the corner of her eye and tells Jessica, "You are in a time-out for taking your sister's cookie. Please get up from the table and sit on the couch." Jessica doesn't budge, so Mom walks over, takes her by the arm, and nudges her out of the kitchen. Jessica sits on the couch but continues to argue from afar why she shouldn't be in time-out. Mom ignores all of it. Jessica takes a break from the rant and her mother uses the opportunity to see if she is ready to come out. Mom walks to the couch and asks Jessica if she knows why she went into time-out. Jessica says yes. Mom tells Jessica to go apologize to her sister for taking her cookie. Jessica apologizes begrudgingly. Mom and Kate accept the apology. Now Mom immediately tries to reengage Jessica by asking her if she wants to do some painting after lunch. Jessica gets excited and starts to talk about what she wants to paint. Mom tells Jessica that she is looking forward to seeing what she makes.

I imagine some of you think that your child would never easily go into time-out. Here is how to handle it when the child doesn't stay in the time-out spot:

Samantha is harassing her brother Tom, who is quietly doing his homework. Dad tells his daughter to leave Tom alone. Samantha hears her dad but thinks this is a funny game. Her brother is bigger and stronger, and the only way she can really get to him is to annoy him. It is working beautifully. He is getting frustrated. Dad tells Samantha to leave her brother alone or she will have a time-out. Right away, Samantha tests Dad by kicking her brother under the table.

Dad already gave one warning, so he says, "You are in a time-out. Go sit on the step." Samantha tries to argue. She says she didn't do anything. Without any show of anger, Dad takes his daughter by the hand and walks her to the step. Then he strolls away. Samantha decides to rise and go back to the kitchen. She stands in the doorway trying to get Dad's attention.

Normally, this would throw Dad into a power struggle. But, in using Ignore it!, he simply averts his gaze and pretends to be busy opening the mail. Now Samantha starts singing at the top of her lungs. Still, Dad ignores her. Samantha is beside herself that no one is paying attention. "I'm not on the step," she says. "I'm not on the step. I'm not on the step." Since Samantha isn't doing her time-out, Dad continues to ignore her. He literally turns his back on her. But he is listening.

Eventually, Samantha decides to give up. She sits quietly on the floor for a minute. Hearing the pause in Samantha's behavior, Dad says, "Samantha, I put you in a time-out because you were interfering with your brother trying to get his work done. If you are ready to leave him alone, you can come out of time-out." Samantha says she is ready. Dad tells her that she can practice the piano or read for a bit until her mom comes home for dinner. Samantha decides to play the piano. After one song, Dad compliments Samantha on her playing.

Both of these scenarios show how time-out and Ignore it! are a match made in heaven. The key to a successful time-out, though, is to remember to Ignore it!. That's the hardest part.

Tips for a Successful Time-Out

- No talking to the child during time-out.
- Keep time-out minutes to a minimum.
- Reengage as soon as the child is ready.
- Avoid eye contact.
- Don't allow any pleasurable activities during time-out.
- Follow through with time-out once it is initiated. Don't allow any arguing or fleeing to obviate the time-out.
- Location should be boring—and never stimulating.
- Location and time-out should not be scary.
- If the child happily goes into time-out, don't engage. This is just another form of manipulation.
- If you cannot walk the child into a time-out location, then withdraw all attention and distractions where you are. Turn off televisions and remove toys.
- If the child destroys property while in a time-out, don't address it at all until the child is calm and the time-out is finished. At that point, in a very calm voice, say, "I am happy to see you have calmed down. Here is a garbage bag. Please clean up your mess."
- Any noise by you (think sucking teeth or grunting) or even a facial expression conveys a message and acts as reinforcement for the child.
- Time-out will be effective only if all attention (reinforcement) is withdrawn. If a sibling is conspiring with or giggling at the child in time-out, it will not work.

CHAPTER 7

Ignore It! in Public

A LMOST EVERY PARENT I know has a nightmarish airplane story involving a child, some screaming and—inevitably—growls and glares. I've sure had my share over the years, but one in particular stands out. Back in 2008, when my son was two, we took a flight from New York to West Palm Beach, Florida. Emmett was strapped into his car seat for takeoff, and it became immediately (and painfully) clear that he wasn't digging the seat. He wanted out. Unfortunately, toddlers can't simply roam freely on a 747, and especially not during takeoff. So, seeing that walking was not an option, my son proceeded to kick the seat in front of him. POP, POP, POP! Of course, within seconds the woman sitting before us spun around and flashed *The Look*. You know whereof I speak—rolling eyes, sighing, tsk-tsking. I felt awful, and firmly told my son, "No, you can't kick her seat. Stop it!" (Admittedly, it was as much for her as him.)

Emmett continued to kick. It was a game for him. I tried again with the lecture and also by restraining him with my hands. I thought if I held his feet down and told him, "No!" in a firm voice, he would just give up. Yeah, right. With my hand pressing against his shins, Emmett commenced with a Pavarotti-level scream that caused 250 heads to swivel toward us. It was the lowest of the lowest of the lows.

I was mortified and furious. Instead of finding a productive way to handle my feelings, I took it out on my son. I grabbed his legs and pushed them away. I snarled at him. I grunted. All to no avail. Not only was he continuing to kick, but now I was ashamed of my behavior toward him. How could I have let strangers affect my parenting in such a way? What in the world was I doing?

Realizing that I was getting nowhere with my son, I decided to chat it up with the lady sitting in front of us. I gently tapped her shoulder and apologized for my son's kicking. As soon as I did this, I regretted it. I'd pretty much sold Emmett out for kindness points. The kid was two. He was irrational. He was frustrated and didn't enjoy being on the plane. For goodness' sake, I didn't enjoy being on the plane, either. So why did this need an apology? Isn't this normative behavior for a two-year-old on a plane?

Well, at least the woman immediately forgave me—even offered a chocolate cookie.

Oh, wait. No, she didn't. In the most condescending of tones, she explained that her children never, ever acted in such an untoward manner. They were perfect angels at all times, the finest offspring in all the land. She wrapped up the scolding by offering some (100 percent unsolicited) advice. She told me—bluntly—to act like the parent and control my son. Then she turned away, content in her successful flogging of a humiliated mother. I was devastated, and I sulked and quietly cried for the remainder of the plane ride.

With me still feeling the sting from my scolding, we walked out of the airport—kids and luggage in tow. And then it hit me. I will never see that mean lady again. What did I care if she thought I was a terrible parent? Furthermore, just because some-one calls me a terrible parent doesn't mean I actually am one. She doesn't know my life. She only saw one tiny snippet of my par-enting ability. Her scorn made me do and say things that I oth-erwise wouldn't have. If I were alone when my son started to lose it, I would have handled it differently. Her opinion shouldn't have affected my parenting at that moment or any other. This revelation—as simple as it may sound—changed my life.

I don't have to answer to others for my parenting decisions. Unless I am abusive or neglectful, I can parent how *I* see fit. My neighbors and parents and grandparents don't have to approve. The grocery store clerk can roll her eyes all she wants. At the end of the day, I am the one going home with my son and daughter. I am the one who will have to deal with their behav-ior. Once I realized my son was kicking, what I should have done was Ignore it!. Well, mostly Ignore it!. Yes, the boy was frustrated, and he was expressing that. But I reinforced his be-havior, and that made him do it more. I should have held his feet down or removed him from the seat to save the woman from his kicking. What I should *not* have done was provide near-constant attention and verbal recognition of his behavior.

In 2016, JetBlue acknowledged how tough flying can be on every passenger—big or little—and created a one-time promo-tion for Mother's Day. At the beginning of the flight, an atten-dant announced on the loudspeaker that: "Every time a baby on this flight cries you will receive 25 percent off your next JetBlue flight. In other words, four cries is equivalent to a round-trip ticket." Cue the cheers. Excited (and somewhat perverse) travelers waited in anticipation for the first cry.

Inevitably, four babies wailed away on the flight and all on board received a free future trip. While this was a sweet gimmick, it also shined a light on the uphill battle parents face when parenting in public. In order for parents of little ones to gain a smidge of understanding, travelers had to be paid—handsomely, I might add—to be tolerant of babies doing what is normal for babies. The trouble is the vast majority of people in the real world aren't as lucky as the passengers on the special JetBlue flight. They receive no benefit for accepting children being children.

Since strangers routinely shame and judge parents based on their children's behavior, it is incumbent upon parents to learn how to deal with these watchful eyes. This chapter is all about how to manage difficult behavior while in public.

Ignoring the Chatter

Before focusing on ignoring our children in public, it's vital we talk about how to ignore the voices of others who try to negatively influence our parenting choices. Modern-day parents are often under a microscope. No one is parenting in privacy. We have smartphones and video cameras on us at all times. We tweet and use Facebook and share our opinions hourly (or, in the case of the Kardashians, every 2.3 seconds). There is little escape from the watchful public eye. And, because of that, there is little escape from shaming.

The stay-at-home moms are inspecting the working moms to see if they are making it to the school trips or doing enough on the PTA. The working moms are keenly observing to see signs of unraveling in the stay-at-home group. Breast-feeders boast while bottle-feeders cower self-consciously in the corner. Those who can afford to live strictly on an organic diet and shop only at Whole Foods snub their noses at those who—either by choice or because of financial constraints—don't live similarly. There are cosleepers and attachment parents who are disgusted by parents who put their kids in day care or aren't at their child's beck and call every moment.

Heaven forbid you get caught in the news or on social media parenting in a way others find questionable. Watch out, because the wrath will be swift and ruthless. Consider what happened to Matt and Melissa Graves of Elkhorn, Nebraska.

In June 2016, the couple took their three children to Disney World and stayed at the Grand Floridian Resort & Spa in Orlando. While wading in an on-property lagoon, their toddler was grabbed by an alligator. Both parents were present and the father tried to wrestle his child out of the alligator's teeth, but was unsuccessful. After the boy was discovered dead, some parents wasted no time shaming this family—as if the tragedy of losing a son weren't enough.

One person tweeted: "An alligator being an alligator. Parent's [*sic*] not being parents." It was retweeted 2,300 times. Another lovely know-it-all wrote: "Oh great, more innocent animals being killed because of piss poor parenting. Stop the world. I want to get off." And yet another kind soul opined: "I'm not sad about a 2yo being eaten by a gator bc his daddy ignored signs."

If parents whose child was taken from them by an alligator at a Disney property while the parents stood right next to the child garner no sympathy from watchful eyes, you can bet you won't, either, when your misstep happens.

Even the most insignificant parental decision is up for debate. Country singer Jana Kramer found this out the hard way when she posted an innocuous picture showing a supermarket conveyer belt covered with baby food jars. The caption simply read, "And it begins. #babyfood." Surely Jana didn't expect the Twitter backlash. . . .

- "Make your own!!! Don't buy jars. Yes they're convenient but not as nutritious as mummy's home made"
- "Make your own. It's cheaper and way healthier ;)"
- "Make your own it'll save money and it's better for her"
- "My sister made her own baby food. Much healthier and now my nephew is almost five won't touch processed food"
- "So easy to make your own! Steam and purée pretty much any fruit or veggie. Great way to avoid pesky preservatives!"

Did these people mean well? I don't know. Maybe. But the posts read like passive-aggressive tirades. Luckily, Kramer refused to take their shaming to heart. She responded to the criticism by posting a picture of a handwritten note saying, "Dear Mommy-Shamers, Unless you are Jolie's doctor, her father, or her mom, do <u>NOT</u> tell me how to raise my child, or how to feed her. Sincerely, Jolie's <u>MOM</u>."

From Jana Kramer we can all learn a lot. It is all too easy to hear these kind of comments and take them personally. Many a parent would internalize the rants about jarred food, feel horribly subpar, and, before long, order a $500 baby-food maker on Amazon Prime. That's how it happens. Subtly but surely. We are disgraced, and as a result we make alterations to the way we raise our offspring. The problem: parenting that works for one family doesn't necessarily work for another.

Donald W. Winnicott was an English pediatrician and psychoanalyst in the 1950s. His theory of the transitional object is why all kids today have a lovey. It's meant to be a substitute love object to help children feel safe and secure when their parents aren't near. Winnicott is also known for his concept of the "good enough mother." He believed that the way to be a good mother is to be a good enough mother. (Remember Winnicott worked in England in the 1950s, when mothers were the primary caretakers. You can now substitute "parent" for "mother.") What he meant was that children don't need perfect parents. Children are far better off with imperfect parents. Dealing with imperfections in their mothers and fathers prepares children to adapt to the harsh external realities in life.

Winnicott knew parents weren't perfect. And what's even better is he recognized that the shortcomings actually resulted in better outcomes for kids and parents. Keep this in mind whenever you feel the competitive pull of parenthood. The next time someone on an airplane flashes the ol' dirty look, you should hear, *You are good enough, and that is better than perfect.* When your child is throwing a fit in the checkout line at Target, think the same thing. And if your child falls off the playground jungle gym at the exact moment you decide to check your iPhone, don't fret. You are good enough.

How to Manage Parenting in Public

- Don't take it all too seriously.
- Laugh if you are having a bad day.

- Remember, you will probably never see these people again.
- Strangers aren't raising your child. You are!

Ignore It! in Public

All of this watching and judging makes ignoring kids in public pretty stressful. It is exceedingly difficult to disregard the scorn from onlookers, especially when it looks like you are ignoring a needy child. But the scorn isn't the only challenge of ignoring in public. Ignore it! only works if *all* attention is withdrawn from the child for her inappropriate behavior. Sometimes people observing a crying child get involved and that acts as enough behavioral reinforcement.

Here's an example: When my daughter was five, she was caught stealing cookies after she was told she couldn't have any more. As a punishment, my husband and I decided there would be no dessert for a week. The sentence progressed without a hitch until we attended a birthday party for our friend Louise's son, Jonathan.

Louise is Italian (an important detail) and a ridiculously lavish party planner. Being a proud Italian, she always has the most amazing food and desserts at her events. At Jonathan's party there was a cotton candy machine, incredible-looking Italian cookies, a chocolate fountain, Rice Krispies treats, and barrels of candy free for the taking. Well, my daughter was apoplectic. I felt terrible for her, but we stuck to our guns. We just let her cry it out and ignored her antics at the party. It was the only way.

But then Louise's grandmother saw my daughter sobbing. She came over concerned, and said, "No one should be crying at this party." We explained why our daughter was upset, but ol' Grandma had none of that. She took my daughter by the hand and walked her over to the dessert table. My daughter wasn't sure what to do. Should she take the dessert from the nice grandma? She looked back at us with apprehensive but hopeful eyes. I had to go fetch my daughter from the clutches of this adoring woman, which induced a new round of hysteria. This time, the crying reached a whole new level. Why? Because my daughter knew people were watching and were ready to intervene on her behalf. Unfortunately for my daughter, our resolve was strong, and she was permitted no dessert.

This is exactly what makes ignoring in public tricky. In order for Ignore it! to work, you have to remove all reinforcers and benefits for the behavior. With some careful preparation and practice, this can be overcome.

Start at Home

Ignoring a screaming or very annoying child is difficult. It takes practice, despite seeming like it would be easy. Our human nature pushes us to respond to crying, yelling, nudging, etc. Before you even think of ignoring while out in public, you must first perfect the practice at home. Make sure you are able to really ignore all of your child's attempts to rope you in. Can you turn away from a kid begging for just one more minute of television? Do fork tapping or annoying noises not affect you anymore? (Okay, at least not as much.) Have you seen a decrease in the frequency or intensity of some of the targeted behaviors? If so, you are ready to try ignoring in public. Don't rush it, though. Remember, it would be worse to start ignoring, but then respond when your child ramps up the undesirable behavior. When you Ignore it! but then intervene when the behavior gets worse, you just teach the child to try harder to receive what he wants. The parent is essentially guaranteeing the behavior to stick around. So make sure you are *really* ready.

Plan Ahead

To ensure you are ready and prepared for the difficult task of ignoring in public, plan ahead. Think of a few locations that are typical pitfalls for you and your child. Target and the supermarket are popular locations for a parent-child tug-of-war. Gift shops, the car, and a relative's house are also good places to start. Once you decide what's the best spot to begin, gear up before you go. Review the steps. Remember **I Like Relaxed Re**ading. Say it a few times (even aloud) so you don't forget what to do.

Ignore It! Review

Ignore: Make no response or noise at all. Withdraw all attention from the child.

Listen: Listen carefully so that you can reengage as soon as the child stops the behavior.

Reengage: Quickly engage.

Repair: Enforce any cleanup or apology that's needed.

Next, imagine yourself ignoring your whining child in the store. Close your eyes and visualize the watchful strangers.

Picture the whispers and dirty looks. Blow it all off. Focus on your child and envision yourself telling these observant, "helpful" strangers, "I've got this." Now picture yourself not giving a hoot. Tell yourself you are good enough and reaffirm to yourself that you can do this.

If you go to a location that is typically a stumbling block and your child behaves beautifully, don't be disappointed that you didn't get a chance to Ignore it!. Instead, make sure to praise your child for good behavior. Then gear up for another time to test Ignore it! in public.

A Time and Place

There are places where you shouldn't Ignore it!. Small restaurants, your grandparents' seventieth wedding anniversary party, or your older child's graduation ceremony would not be ideal spots for Ignore it!.

Sometimes there are just too many outside influences around who might provide the attention that you withdraw. In those cases, at the same time you are ignoring, someone else is reinforcing the behavior. This can lead to great frustration on your part (worse than the frustration of the behavior in the first place). So skip the ignoring until you can be sure to control the outsiders looking in. Instead, use other discipline or prevention techniques to manage behavior (I'll discuss these techniques in Chapters 10 and 11).

Another time when I wouldn't Ignore it! in public is if you are the only grown-up watching multiple children. For example, it is probably too challenging to look like you are ignoring a misbehaving four-year-old while simultaneously watching an active toddler. Again, find another way to discipline or skip it this time.

Sometimes the location where the behavior starts isn't ideal, but you can make a few alterations to complete Ignore it!. Elizabeth and John decided to take the kids out for a nice dinner. This was after a neighborhood birthday party, which included copious amounts of sweets. Dinner went well. But when John said "no thanks" to the waiter's suggestion of dessert, Maya kicked off negotiations. John explained why he'd said no, but Maya kept at it with an increasing audio level. Soon she was yelling that John and Elizabeth were the meanest parents.

The restaurant was tiny and the outburst was clearly ruining the meals of other patrons. Ignoring at this restaurant wouldn't be fair to the neighboring diners. So instead of ignoring right there, John excused himself from the table and took Maya outside. He said nothing to Maya. He just waited with her on the sidewalk until she stopped asking about dessert and fussing about his decision. As soon as she quieted for a few seconds, John said he was ready to go back into the restaurant. He and Elizabeth had been practicing Ignore it! at home. Maya realized what was going on. From her experience, once the parents started to ignore her, the jig was up. She wasn't going to win, so she moved on fairly quickly.

Maya and John walked back into the restaurant and sat down with the rest of the family. People were staring. They wanted another look at the loudest child. John and Elizabeth could see this, but they didn't care. They grinned to each other with pride; they had come one step closer to eliminating Maya's negotiating once and for all.

Handle the ignoring location as you would a time-out. Find

a place where ignoring makes more sense. This includes a place where there are fewer people, where others won't be inconvenienced because of your child's behavior, or where you can step away from your child to look like you are ignoring him/her. I have done this in a parking lot, in the car, on the sidewalk, and in the bathroom of a restaurant.

Putting It All Together

Nine-year-old Calvin is used to getting what he wants. When his parents, Vinnie and Sheila, tried to deny him, he would throw a massive tantrum. Usually, his mother became embarrassed or exasperated and would give in. Over time, this became a way of life for Calvin and his folks. Calvin's parents felt like they were being held hostage by a monster in a child's body. After hearing about Ignore it!, they learned that they were actually encouraging Calvin's behavior by giving him attention and responding to the tantrums. They decided to try Ignore it! on a family trip to a science museum. In the gift shop, Calvin asked for a game. After his parents said no, he began to throw a huge fit. There was yelling, screaming, and crying. Calvin's parents could see people glaring at them. But, feeling confident after understanding why Ignore it! works, they quietly walked slightly away from Calvin. They kept an eye on him, but they pretended to look at some books. Other shoppers were aghast. Calvin was confused. Vinnie and Sheila felt a momentary pang of self-doubt. But then they remembered these strangers weren't raising their son. To hell with them.

This kind of tantrum usually worked in a jiffy for Calvin. But when he looked up after screaming, he could see the faces of the other shoppers. Suddenly, *he* was embarrassed. He then saw that his parents were paying him no mind, so he got up and meekly asked if they could leave the store. Calvin's parents were elated and, of course, were ready to depart. Calvin's mother put her arm around her son's shoulders and sauntered lovingly toward the exit. Over time, Calvin steadily toned down the level and frequency of his tantrums. Instead of giving Calvin attention for his inappropriate behavior, his parents were now focusing on catching him being good. Calvin liked that and was working hard at earning points to get a game from the museum.

Vinnie and Sheila did a lot right at the science museum. They did what they knew they needed to do to break Calvin's habit of tantruming when he didn't get what he wanted. They really wanted to be able to go places with Calvin without major meltdowns. This challenge was important to them, so they remained focused on the steps. They did this in the store together, which provided them each with some much-needed support, and they didn't let the onlookers derail their plan. Vinnie and Sheila also positively reengaged Calvin as soon as they could. Calvin responded to their energy and completely left the tantrum behind.

Important Points to Remember

- Strangers aren't raising your child; you are. Their opinions are irrelevant.
- A good enough parent is better than a perfect one.
- Start Ignore it! in public only after practicing at home and creating a plan for ignoring while out.

CHAPTER 8

This Isn't Working. Everything Is Getting Worse.

THROUGHOUT MY CAREER as a parenting coach, I've uttered many sentences to many clients. Yet the one nobody—and I mean absolutely, positively nobody—wants to hear is this: "It gets worse before it gets better." Parents don't want to hear that their child-rearing problems will turn darker before the light arrives. Nope. They crave immediate answers and immediate resolution. They want crying to stop, healthy eating to begin, eight-hour sleep stretches to commence ASAP.

Believe me, I get it. Truly, I do.

Alas, reality can be a bit harsh. And even with Ignore it!, things can get worse (though briefly—*I promise*) before they get better. Here's an example to explain whereof I speak:

Remember when you were a student in elementary school? There was always that one kid who couldn't sit in his seat when he knew the answer to a question. He was the real-world sibling of Arnold Horshack from *Welcome Back, Kotter*: the annoying kid who would "oooh" and "ahhhhhh" and wave his hand around and snap his fingers and clap and all but fall from his chair to get the teacher's attention.

Well, Jodie, who was a teacher friend of mine, had this exact kind of kid in her classroom. Georgie wildly raised his hand because he learned that, even if he got scolded, the display worked. Georgie caught the teacher's attention and often was called on to answer the question. But sometimes Jodie didn't call on him. Instead, she would say, "Georgie, I won't acknowledge you if you aren't sitting quietly when you raise your hand." Even though Jodie wouldn't call on him, she was sending attention his way.

I introduced my friend to Ignore it!, and she quickly recognized her mistake in calling on Georgie when he used inappropriate means to become noticed. Every time she so much as glanced at Georgie during his outbursts, she reinforced his behavior. So Jodie decided to implement Ignore it!. The very next time Georgie or any other student became shifty in his seat and waved his hand around wildly, she would ignore him.

The next day Georgie got excited again because he knew the answer to the question. Just like always, he raised his hand exuberantly. But this time he didn't receive his teacher's attention. *Something must be wrong*, Georgie surely thought.

He grew rowdier and more aggressive in trying to show the teacher he knew the answer. Jodie still didn't notice him, and she called on the quiet girl three seats to the left. Later in the day, the scenario replayed itself. Georgie did his all to get his teacher to call on him, and she pretended he didn't exist. He jumped up and down. He loudly called her name. He begged.

He pleaded. When she seemed like she didn't see him, he started jumping up and down in his seat.

He was saying the teacher's name, "Mrs. Jones! Mrs. Jones! MRS. JONES!" over and over again. But oddly she still didn't see or hear him. Georgie couldn't figure out what was going on, so he stood up and blurted out the answer. Jodie, practicing Ignore it!, continued to ignore Georgie. He was perplexed, and his behavior got even worse. He yelled with increased frequency. He banged on his desk. My friend called me and said Ignore it! wasn't working. "It's getting harder and harder." She sighed. "I can't handle this."

"No," I said. "Trust me—it's working like a charm." Indeed, several weeks later she called again. "I can't believe it," she said, "but Georgie is a changed student."

This chapter explains why sometimes behavior worsens with Ignore it!, how to handle it—and why it will get better.

Quickly.

Extinction Burst

When using Ignore it!, behavior can sometimes get worse for a short period before it improves. That is known as an extinction burst. It is actually a well-researched phenomenon. Studies show that the targeted behavior you are ignoring can increase in magnitude, frequency, and duration before improving.

Here's a pretty solid way to explain it in adult terms: You go for a long run on a ninety-degree summer day. Over the last mile you're dreaming of the icy-cold Gatorade that awaits once you finish. You reach the vending machine, place a $1 bill into the slot, and make your selection. Only nothing comes out. So you tap-tap-tap-tap all the buttons, and you tap-tap-tap some more.

Still nothing. You feel your blood pressure rising. Sweat is trickling down your forehead. You bang the front of the machine, hoping something will jolt into place and deliver your desperately needed beverage. Still nothing. Man, are you angry! So in one last frantic attempt you kick the machine as you walk away. Alas, no Gatorade appears.

Let's break down the vending machine example so you can see exactly how this relates to Ignore it!.

> **Established behavior:** Putting money into the vending machine (in parenting terms, think whining)
> **Positive reinforcement received:** Getting a drink (think a Snickers bar purchased at Target checkout)
> **Ignore it! initiated:** Established behavior is no longer rewarded. Thus, money is put into machine but no reward—the drink. (Parent begins to ignore whining.)
> **Extinction burst:** Angry attempts to get the machine to work

If this scenario happened to you, what do you think you would do on your next run? You might make alternative arrangements. Maybe you pack a drink in a cooler or figure out the location of the nearest 7-Eleven. But what if you didn't learn your lesson just yet? Imagine again that you take the same long run in the same heat. You reach the vending machine, and you put in your money. Guess what happens? Nothing. Once again your drink doesn't come out. You are incensed now, but not merely at the machine. You are probably a bit furious that you made the same mistake. In one last-ditch effort to get a drink, you punch the vending machine.

Your fist throbs with pain, but nothing comes out. After two failures, I'm fairly certain you won't put money into it again. Or, as the old saying goes, "Fool me once, shame on you. Fool me twice, shame on me." You will have learned to find a new way to deal with your thirst and you will have learned that kicking a vending machine is not going to produce a drink, no matter how thirsty you may be.

The vending machine situation is typical of the extinction burst you may see when beginning Ignore it!. It should be viewed as a normal consequence to years of rewarding undesirable behavior. The good news is this period is usually brief and can be overcome easily.

Here are some typical ways an extinction burst is exhibited:

- More frequent tantrums
- Longer tantrums
- Louder tantrums
- More cursing or mean language
- Increased usage of physical force
- More hitting
- Possible biting
- Throwing toys and other objects
- Destruction of property
- An introduction of new problem behaviors
- Self-injurious behaviors such as headbanging (These require additional help from a counselor proficient in applied behavioral analysis. See Appendix D for resources.)

- Dangerous behavior toward the caregiver (Also seek outside help.)

Remember that the extinction burst can be an increase in intensity, duration, and frequency. A child who ordinarily throws approximately three tantrums a day might have five or six or seven or *even eight* during an extinction burst. The tantrums might be angrier and more aggressive.

Last, if the child usually quiets after having a tantrum for five to ten minutes, those tantrums now may last twenty to even forty minutes. But—*and this is an important "but"*—right after the last-ditch effort of a tantrum, the behavior will practically disappear. For some children, the targeted behavior will completely vanish, never to be seen again. For others, the behavior will be drastically improved. Will your four-year-old *never* have a tantrum again? I highly doubt that. But your experience as a parent will be much improved by marginalizing once-regular explosions.

Extinction: The process of eliminating or reducing a conditioned response by not reinforcing it. This is the essence of Ignore it!.
Extinction burst: A temporary increase in the frequency, duration, or magnitude of the undesired behavior after the initiation of Ignore it!.

Stay the Course

One of the problems with the extinction burst is that it fools people. Parents recognize a problem, seek to fix it, and choose a course of action. Then, with the first sign of trouble, they back off and surrender. Parents immediately assume that their intervention is a mistake because behavior is worse. That setback isn't just a major bummer. It's demoralizing, and teaches children that they can make their parents change their minds by behaving horribly. This sets parents up for an even harder time parenting and implementing changes.

Take the example of a child who has difficulty walking away from video games. Mom and Dad decide that if their son, Jamie, doesn't turn off his Xbox 360 when asked before dinner, he will lose the game system for the rest of the evening. The first few times Mom and Dad try to enforce the new rule, their son turns angry. He calls his folks names, but they just Ignore it!. On the third day of taking away the video game, Jamie goes haywire. Dad is still at work, so Mom is trying to ignore Jamie on her own. He argues, complains, mocks her clothes and her haircut and asks aloud whether she's gained fifteen or twenty pounds this month. Then, as a capper, he starts throwing game pieces at her. One piece hits Mom right below the eye. At that, Mom reaches her breaking point and says, "Fine, play all night if you want. I don't care anymore!" Then she storms off to her bathroom for a good cry.

Mom is human, and she took just about all she could take. But unfortunately, Mom made life much more difficult for herself in the future. She might have given up in that one moment, but the repercussions of her change of plan will be more severe and long-lasting.

Even though the extinction burst can be quite stressful, it is usually short-lived. The extinction burst lasts as long as it takes for the child to receive the message: the behavior is not effective in producing the expected payoffs. When a child notices that the parent will no longer reward bad behavior, there can be a backlash. Often children are disappointed and furious that the rules of their relationship have changed. Imagine that your work hours have always been eight to four. Then one day your boss tells you the new shift is eleven to seven, including weekends. You'd be miffed, right?

Same here with Ignore it!. And expecting the extinction burst will help parents stay on the Ignore it! path. Furthermore, the extinction burst should be seen as confirmation that Ignore it! *is* having an impact. The child is reacting, which means he sees the change. All good news. Stay the course!

Bursts and Bursts and Bursts

One more issue needs to be broached in regard to extinction bursts. Sometimes there is a burst in one behavior. When that behavior is quelled, there can be a burst in another. And then another. For example . . .

Meet Rachel. She was the whiniest child of all time. She whined when she was given only twenty French fries. She whined when she couldn't have lemonade. She even whined when her mother took her to the paint-your-own pottery store to paint a small figurine. Rachel wanted to know why she couldn't paint a plate or a bowl or the big figures. Mom said no. But "no" never meant "no" for Rachel. She whined and whined and whined.

Know a child like Rachel? The odds are high that you do.

Rachel finally met her match when her mom started ignoring her whining. Mom felt a sense of relief that she didn't have to address every one of Rachel's complaints. Mom excitedly began to ignore Rachel's objections. As soon as Rachel stopped complaining, Mom knew to quickly reengage her.

Each time Mom began to ignore whining, Rachel was shocked. She normally whined and complained and nagged, and nine times out of ten, she received what she wanted. It might have been an extra fry or the lemonade. It might even have been negative attention, which is fine by Rachel. Because when Rachel is being yelled at, her mom's focus is on her and not her mother's work or cell phone or Rachel's brother.

Anyway, when Rachel got a whiff that her normal tricks were no longer working, she became livid but also remained calm and decided to redouble her efforts. She thought if only she whined more, she would wear her mother out. Then her mother would break down and give in, just like always. Rachel's behavior turned worse. A lot worse. Her complaining was louder, nastier, and more intrusive.

Rachel's mom knew to expect the extinction burst. However, Rachel's case was more complex than the average child. Rachel had been manipulating her parents for many years. Because of the length of time that her parents rewarded her undesirable behavior, it would take longer to eradicate all signs of the behavior.

Figure 1 shows exactly how Rachel exhibited the initial extinction burst. Mom kept a record of the number of times Rachel whined in a day for eight days prior to initiating any changes. Rachel typically had between five and seven incidents a day. On the ninth day, Mom began to Ignore it! and Rachel's behavior spiked in the extinction burst. The next few days were excruciating for Mom. Rachel complained at an Olympic rate.

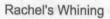

Figure 1: Rachel's Initial Extinction Burst

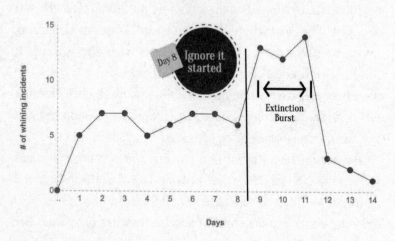

Mom counted at least twelve occurrences on days nine, ten, and eleven. Mom was exhausted, but she kept at it. Amazingly, by day twelve, Rachel's complaining began to recede. From then on there were only one or two occurrences a day. Hooray for Mom! Well, almost. Hold off on the celebration.

While Ignore it! was clearly having an impact on Rachel's whining, other behaviors started to appear. Mom kept track of all inappropriate behavior, and the results can be seen in Figure 2. Rachel became a negotiator. As soon as whining was beginning to be a distant memory, negotiating took its place. Now Rachel was an expert mediator, feeling as if there was nothing she couldn't negotiate her way into and out of. Rachel negotiated like a champ on days thirteen through sixteen.

Mom recognized that the negotiating was merely a replacement behavior for whining. She continued Ignore it! for all the negotiating, and by day seventeen the mediating was nearly gone. Just when Mom was ready to retire Ignore it!, one last extinction burst occurred. The insults arrived. Mom was a bit taken aback. She knew Rachel might get whinier and that the incidents might happen more often. This, though, was uglier than usual. I explained to Mom that the behavior had never reached such a level because her daughter was usually able to manipulate the situation. This was a very difficult phase for Mom, but the previous success with whining and negotiating helped her maintain resolve and focus.

By day twenty-five, almost all of Rachel's objectionable behavior had disappeared. Mom remained vigilant with any remaining whining and negotiating as they occurred. She continued to Ignore it! and the behavior was manageable. Mom

Figure 2: How to Handle the Extinction Burst

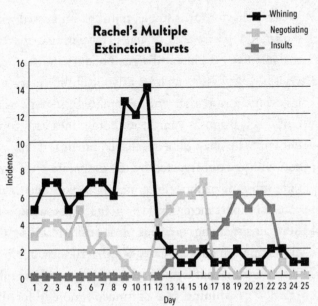

reported an incredible change in her own mood overall. She had anticipated that Rachel would change with Ignore it!, but she didn't believe she would, too. Mom explained she was able to enjoy her time with Rachel in a way she hadn't in years.

The most important point to remember is to ignore all related undesirable behavior that occurs once you begin to Ignore it!. Just keep with the program. And remember that the extinction burst, while exceedingly difficult at times, is proof that your implementation of Ignore it! is making a difference. Hang in there and keep ignoring through the burst. Right after that, the behavior will drastically improve. Wait for it.

Tips to Get Through the Extinction Burst

1. View the extinction burst as a sign that your efforts are being noticed.
2. When behavior turns worse, try to be impressed with your child's perseverance and persistence. It may be maladaptive here but still a good quality in life.
3. Laugh. Okay, not out loud at your child. That's not ignoring it, and that will undoubtedly enrage your child. But laugh in your head. Sometimes kids come out with the most unbelievable comments. Trust me, you will be flabbergasted by the desperate stuff your kids utter. Finding humor will help you keep your cool and not engage when the going gets tough.
4. Stay consistent. Ignore it! is most difficult during the extinction burst. It can be easy to have a slipup. However, consistency ensures that the reward for the

behavior is completely removed. This is what stops the behavior.

5. Make sure you aren't waiting too long to reengage. Some angry behavior could be as a result of a missed opportunity to divert attention. Remember to listen carefully when you are ignoring so that you can reengage as soon as possible.

PART III

CHAPTER 9

Encouraging Good Behavior and the Opposite of Ignoring

The ideal of behaviorism is to eliminate coercion: to apply controls by changing the environment in such a way as to reinforce the kind of behavior that benefits everyone.

—B. F. Skinner

Although it doesn't always seem to be the case, children want to please their parents. Without a second thought, they would choose praise over punishment, commendations over condemnations. Give kids the chance to act correctly, and they almost always will. But how to provide such an opportunity?

Ignore it! solves only part of the parenting puzzle. It helps parents eliminate many of the annoying and frustrating day-to-day behaviors, and that's huge. But there remains a need to increase desirable action. It isn't enough to merely ignore the bad. We need to encourage the good. The underlying principle of Ignore it! is that behavior that is reinforced is more likely to be repeated. Parents are just reinforcing all the wrong behaviors.

Take thirteen-year-old Jeremy, for example. He is chronically late for school because he takes forever to do everything in the morning. His mother, Janie, begs and pleads with him to hurry up. She shouts because once again Jeremy can't find his binder.

Janie runs around the house trying to rush Jeremy out the door before the bus comes. Jeremy yells back, "Where is my binder?" When he misses the bus, Janie drives the boy to school, a scowl glued to her face. "If you miss the bus again," she says, "I'm not going to drive you." But it's a toothless threat, and he knows it. Instead of reinforcing organization, timeliness, and positivity in the mornings, Janie is rewarding all of Jeremy's shortcomings. She gives his rants attention, she picks up the pieces when he isn't ready, and she makes taking the bus completely optional.

Janie says he must catch the bus "or else." But "or else" never comes. She rewards his missing the bus with a comfortable, chauffeured drive to school. Why should Jeremy get his act together when his mother is doing it for him? Plus, as an added bonus, he is seeing his mother run around the house like a pit bull chasing its tail. The vision makes him laugh.

Studies show that extinction (Ignore it!) is much more successful in eliminating undesirable behaviors when combined with positive reinforcement. Furthermore, the potential for an extinction burst (you know, the behavior getting worse before it gets better) is also diminished when reinforcement is applied to appropriate behaviors.

However, it's easier to pay attention to negative than it is to focus on the positive. So if Ignore it! seems difficult, be prepared that giving praise and rewards for sustained good behavior might be harder. But it will be impossible to fully eradicate unwanted behavior without it.

What's the Opposite of Unwanted?

Behavior exists to serve a purpose. Siblings fight to have their parents intervene. A child begs for ice cream because often that begging leads to a double scoop of Rocky Road on a sugar cone. A teen is obnoxious and rude because he wants to be left alone. Parents usually find this behavior unpleasant and thus leave the teen alone. A little girl turns dramatic after even the smallest bump because she craves extra attention. A boy ignores his parents' requests to turn off the television because he knows if he pretends he doesn't hear them he can snag an extra fifteen minutes.

Behavior has function, a reason for existing. That reason is the reward. When parents recognize the rewards children are obtaining through nefarious means and apply those same rewards to appropriate behaviors, the parenting game is forever changed. Inappropriate behavior decreases while desirable behavior increases.

Before we get to how to reward children, we need to know for what we are rewarding them. When parents ask me for help dealing with their children's difficult behaviors, I ask them what behavior they would *like* to see. Parents typically say:

- I want them to behave.
- I want them to listen.
- I want them to stop being rude.
- I want them to stop hitting each other.
- I want them to be neater around the house.
- I want them to stop whining, crying, or negotiating when they don't get what they want.

This list makes perfect sense to me, and the parents' wants are all reasonable. The problem is that these goals aren't attainable in their current format. They are vague and immeasurable. How would a parent know if a child is behaving or listening? What would constitute "being neater"?

Parents need to formulate their desires into concrete, measurable behaviors so they know exactly when to respond with the reward. The best way to start thinking about preferable behavior is to think about the behavior you have been ignoring. Now think of an opposite of that ignored behavior and make sure that could be measured by an observer. For every behavior you would like to eliminate from your parenting experience, you must replace it with a more positive option. The chart below provides a few more examples.

Unwanted Behavior	Opposite Measurable Behavior
Whining	Uses appropriate voice and speech to ask for something
Crying	No tantrum when not given what is wanted
Negotiating	Accepts "no" on the first try
Messy	Keeps clothes off the floor and dirty laundry in hamper
Loud	Speaks in an appropriate indoor voice
Bad table manners	Uses napkin and fork and knife at meals
Rude	Uses "please" and "thank you"
Unpleasant attitude	Goes on family outings without complaining

Think of these behaviors as substitutes for the behavior you've been ignoring. Once you have identified the specific behaviors that you would like to see more frequently, we can move on to consciously planning to reward those behaviors.

Putting the Carrot in Front of the Horse

Rewards act as incentives to perform tasks. There are two ways people are rewarded in life: externally and internally. External reinforcement happens when someone or something provides outside motivation for behavior. Motivation can come in the form of tangible rewards or verbal acknowledgment. Examples are a raise at work, being told "Great job!" or a dollar given for every strong grade on a report card (even grades are a form of external reinforcement). Internal reinforcement is when a person's behavior is motivated from within. Kids play sports because they're fun. That's internal reinforcement. When kids play sports for the trophy or to make Dad proud, that's external reinforcement.

Parents are sometimes hesitant to provide external rewards for behavior because they worry children won't ever learn to be motivated without the reward dangling. This fear is only partially supported by research. When it comes to motivation to do complex, labor intensive and creative tasks, external rewards are less effective and could possibly undermine interest and the quality of the outcomes. Additionally, external incentives can be detrimental when there is already internal motivation for a task. But when there is no interest because tasks are inherently not enjoyable (think cleaning a room or emptying the dishwasher) or there has been a long-standing pattern of misbehavior, it can be necessary to create an external reward as a jump start for good behavior. Let's go back to Jeremy. Right now, he has absolutely no internal motivation to get to school on time. He hates classes and the bus, so his delay tactics are working out perfectly. In order for Mom to motivate

Jeremy to change his behavior, the reward will have to start out externally.

External rewards can also foster internal motivation. Picture an old lady crossing the street. As a teen boy passes, the lady falls down with a truck quickly approaching. The teen rushes into the street, picks the woman up, and carries her to the sidewalk. People see how he risked his own safety to help out this woman, and they congregate around him to offer praise. The woman herself is grateful, and the local chief of police asks the boy to come to the station to accept a Good Samaritan award. A few days later a local newspaper reporter calls to find out more information for an article in the Sunday paper.

Now, why did the boy help the old woman? Do you think he did it so he could become a local hero? Or did he do it because at some point he was taught to look after older people? I can assure you it's the latter. But how did his parents teach him to help older people? Well, they might have shown him by example. But they also probably praised him when he held the door for someone before entering a restaurant. They might have thanked him for helping feed a grandparent who had a stroke. Maybe they gave a smile or a nod or a thumbs-up whenever he showed respect for an adult. The boy's parents provided positive reinforcement (external rewards) each time their son did a nice gesture. In turn, he enjoyed receiving that kind of affirmation, and he continued to be a helpful person. Eventually, the boy learned that being helpful felt good and he motivated himself without expecting any outside affirmation.

Parents can and should provide children with external motivation for good behavior. Rewarding children is a teaching and shaping opportunity, not a luxury that can be skipped. Life is full of outside rewards. So parents should use these types of rewards for their advantage to improve behavior without worry. Properly utilized reinforcement paired with Ignore it! teaches children that behaving appropriately leads to more benefits than acting up.

Positive reinforcement: Providing a benefit for behavior that increases the chances the behavior will occur again

External reinforcement: Behavior that is driven by rewards provided by others

Internal reinforcement: Behavior that is motivated by internal rewards

The Rewards

Rewards can come in four different forms: social, edible, tangible, and experiential (see chart on p. 141 for more examples.) The most basic and stress-free of all rewards are social. These consist of verbal encouragement or nonverbal signs of positive acknowledgment such as a wink, high five, or thumbs-up. Social rewards are easy to administer, readily available, and free. But some kids aren't motivated by social acceptance. Other children might have difficulty recognizing nonverbal social cues, so social rewards can be less effective for them. Last, older children might bristle at the idea of Mom or Dad praising them out in the open. A high five from Dad in public? Um, no thank you. Social rewards, though, work splendidly for children who are eager to please.

Edible rewards are items such as soda, juice, mini-marshmallows or M&M's, gum, and dessert. These rewards are highly motivating and desired by youngsters. Many a toddler has been potty trained with the help of a small sweet treat after a tinkle. However, some parents prefer not to use food as a reward due to potential for increased sugar intake, weight gain, or developing an unhealthy relationship with consumption of less-than-healthy foods. Additionally, edible rewards are less effective when the child already receives sweets.

Tangible prizes for good behavior are items the child can literally hold. Toys, magazines, books, stickers, clothing, LEGOs, Matchbox cars, or art supplies are all good examples. Younger children love tangible objects. Many are collectors by nature. Others simply enjoy snagging something new. Older children also feel deeply motivated in attaining items similar to the ones owned by peers. Trends change quickly, and it can be difficult for teens to keep up. Rewarding them can be exceptionally motivating. However, tangible rewards generally cost money—and, in some cases, a lot of money. A gumball is a quarter. *Madden 2017* is not.

The last type of reward is experiential. These benefits come from doing rather than receiving. Some popular experiential rewards are trips to favorite locations (library, bookstore, park), solo time with a parent or working on a special project, a picnic, a visit to a beloved family member, or cooking an exceptional meal (one can rarely go wrong with taco night).

I love experiential rewards because they serve dual purposes. On the one hand, children are allowed to do something they enjoy, which helps motivate the good behavior. But parents also benefit from the experience, as does the relationship between the parent and child. The downsides of experiential rewards are that they can be difficult to schedule, and they also often aren't free.

Four Types of Rewards

Social	Edible	Tangible	Experiential
Hugs	Soda	Stickers	Picnic
Kisses	Egg cream	Stamps	Snuggle
Verbal acknowledgment	Ice-cream sundae	Temporary tattoos	Bubble bath
Thumbs-up	Ice-cream shake	Matchbox cars	Cooking or baking
Nod	Slurpee	LEGOs	Delayed bedtime
Praise	Kona Ice	Treasure chest	Computer time
A smile	Mini-marshmallows	Magazine	Video game time
High five	M&M's	Book	Trip to library or bookstore
Pat on the back	Candy	Buying a movie	Extra story at bedtime
Wink	Favorite meal at home	Buying songs	Special trip
	Restaurant	Apps	Party
	Pizza	Sporting goods	
		Art supplies	
		New clothing	

Guidelines

There are no hard-and-fast rules to help you decide what is the best reward for your child. But there are a few guidelines that might help.

Rewards are effective only if they are something desired *and* special to the child. In order for a child to be truly motivated by the reward, it must be craved whole-heartedly. Just because your kid digs stickers doesn't mean she'll jump through hoops to attain one. If the child has every single LEGO kit on the market, securing a packet of LEGOs as a reward probably won't be so motivating. It's taken for granted. However, another child who loves LEGOs would be psyched to garner a new piece every time he cleans up his toys without a second warning. The bottom line: find the right reward for the right child.

Rewards must be administered immediately following the behavior. It doesn't work to tuck a child into bed and let him know you were proud for something that happened eight hours earlier. A warm moment with Grandma at eleven a.m. is—in the mind of a young child—an eternity ago by one o'clock. In other words, even if the tangible reward will follow at a later time, make sure to recognize the good behavior using social reinforcement straightaway.

Remember, every behavior is done for a purpose. Think back to the behaviors you identified to Ignore it!. What purpose did those behaviors serve for your child? Was it to generate more attention? Was the negotiating to receive more books at bedtime? Did the kids whine to acquire more toys or dessert? If possible, use that purpose as the reward for the opposite behavior. If your child typically brought forth a buffet of delay tactics at bedtime, reward swiftness for hopping into bed. If the child is in pajamas, teeth brushed, by eight p.m., give her an extra book. It's the same desired reward, only now for the preferred behavior. If your child craves your attention, give it more freely, but only when the behavior warrants it.

Sometimes parents are so eager to improve behavior that they go overboard with the rewards. This is an absolutely awful way to go, because before you can yell, "Who wants some ice cream?" the kids will either be numb to overtures or you'll be broke from overdoing it. Think of the smallest reward that will motivate your child. If a bigger reward is needed, build up to it with smaller rewards (see "token economy" on p. 145).

In order to have children invested in the reward system, provide a few easy opportunities. If children think the behavior is too difficult, they will likely opt out. Begin with only a few desirable behaviors that you would like to see more. (Children can't work on ten behaviors at once. Two to three is more reasonable.) Pick one easy behavior the child already does, but infrequently. Pick one behavior that the child can do but doesn't. And choose one behavior that is developmentally in reach for the child but would be a stretch. It is even better if you find one behavior that the child is guaranteed to have success with, because you will ignore all other behaviors. Take a very rude child who makes loads of demands without a "please" or "thank you." Plan on ignoring all requests that don't have a "please" or "thank you" attached. Respond only if the child asks in an appropriate way. *Then* give the reward.

This way, the child is guaranteed to earn the reward because you will ignore all demands. This produces a win-win for both parent and child. As the child improves at the targeted behavior, you should make the rewards harder to obtain. For example, at first a child scores a reward every time she makes her bed without being asked. But you don't want to reward her for this chore for the rest of her life. So once she starts raking up the rewards, you make the challenge a bit more difficult. Tell her she lands the reward only if she can make her bed for five straight days. Once she completes the task, make certain the new reward is bigger than the last one. Finally, when it is clear the rewards have stopped serving as motivators, offer one final assignment. Something akin to "Make the bed every day without being asked for two weeks and at the end you can have five friends over for a slumber party." Have one final prize for accomplishing the behavior. Make a big, excited stink about how amazing she has become and then take it off of the reward list. Of course, you should continue to provide verbal or social praise as appropriate for the task.

Sometimes children are not ready for the goal behavior you have in mind. For example, siblings who fight the second they get in the car will never make it far without battling. If you set a goal that they sit together peacefully for twenty minutes, well, it's not going to happen. You're setting them up for failure. Instead, break it down into attainable mini-goals. If they can't sit for five minutes without an argument, start with four. Similarly, if you want your child to cook dinner, don't start off demanding a five-course gourmet meal. Too overwhelming. Make a mini-goal of piecing together a salad or a side dish. Then build on that once it is achieved.

There is one cardinal rule of positive reinforcement and rewards: *Once a reward is earned, it cannot be taken away*. Often, parents and children get excited to kick off a reward system. But inevitably, unwanted behavior rears its head and parents turn angry. In a moment of frustration, without tools to help, parents take away earned rewards. Nothing—absolutely nothing—sabotages efforts to improve good behavior more than this. The quickest way to have your child abandon the reward system is to take away points or stars or whatever you are offering. Why bother trying to be good if whenever there is a slipup, those rewards can be taken away? All positivity of the plan is undermined, and often the child feels it isn't worth it. If I made a mistake at work, my boss couldn't possibly take back the money I'd already earned. It's the same with rewards. So, once again, remember the cardinal rule: never take away a reward that was earned but not yet consumed or purchased. Ever!

Token Economy and the Reward Chart

A behavior modification program providing children with theoretical or real tokens that can be exchanged later for something else is called a token economy. In school, my son earns imitation dollars that he can exchange for privileges such as pizza for lunch or walking to a local shop with his teacher. These dollars are rewards for quality behavior. At home kids can earn points, stickers, stars, LEGOs, pennies, marbles, or tickets that are traded in for a bigger prize.

Parents provide several options for prizes, some with small value if children want more immediate rewards. Other prizes take time to earn enough tokens because they are worth more.

For example, maybe five tokens represent an extra story at bedtime or ten more minutes of video game play. But fifty tokens result in a special night out for hibachi at the Japanese steak house. Token economies are just like the real economy. I work for money. But money alone doesn't do anything for me unless I trade it in for food or housing or a car. Having the money is the primary reward. But spending it is the secondary gain.

Token economies provide many important advantages for kids and their parents. First, tokens can be awarded immediately, anywhere, anytime. This is important because in order to strengthen the connection between the behavior and the reinforcement, it needs to happen right after the behavior. Tokens allow parents to have children work up to the special rewards while still providing some reinforcement. The token, in and of itself, is a reward. While it can't be enjoyed on its own, it acts as a placeholder. Tokens are strong motivators for older children and can effectively provide impulse to do harder or less desirable tasks.

Variety in rewards can be vital for children who lose interest. Say you have been rewarding a child for staying all night in his bed with a small cup of Froot Loops cereal in the morning. After some time, the child inevitably tires of the snack. He would much rather skip the reward and head into your bed. Tokens allow for frequently changing rewards based entirely on what is of interest to the child.

To begin using a token economy, make a list of rewards with increasing value (either monetary or time). Then assign a value for each reward. In other words, how many tokens (tickets, stickers, whatever) will the child be required to earn before being able to trade for the reward? Older children should be asked to help compile the list so they have a vested interest. For younger children who can't read, find pictures of the desired items and paste them on the chart (see sample chart below).

(Note: All of the following charts are available for download at www.TheFamilyCoach.com.)

Sample Token Economy Value Chart for Young Children

Picture	Reward	Point Value
	M&M's (1 for each point)	1
	5 mintues later bedtime	5
	A trip out for ice cream	20
	$10 to spend at a toy store	50

Connecting the Dots

Once you have decided upon rewards, and once you have identified positive behaviors to work on, you are ready to create the chart. There are many premade charts available online.

However, I have found that they aren't so customizable as I would like. It is easy enough to make one that meets your needs using Microsoft Word or Excel or the old-fashioned way with markers and paper. I will review a few samples that I used when my children were much younger.

Let's start with Emmett's chart. My son was five when we used the nonreader chart (see p. 149). Because he was young, we focused upon only three behaviors to improve: cleaning his room, putting away toys, and reading a book on his own. These specific behaviors were selected because they represented the opposite of the problem behaviors. Instead of nagging Emmett to put his toys away, we focused our energy on rewarding him when he listened. The sample token economy value chart explained pictorially to Emmett what he could earn for each star on his chart. (I went to the local drugstore and bought hundreds of star stickers.) Emmett was so into getting rewards that he would run to his chart to put the stars on it.

Emmett's Sample Nonreader Chart

	Monday	Tuesday	Wednesday	Thursday	Friday	Saturday	Sunday
Clean Room							
Put Toys Away							
Read Books Yourself							
Totals							

My daughter, Casey, was nine at the time. She could read, so her chart looked a little different (see p. 150). She could also handle working on a few behaviors at one time. Again, the behaviors on her chart were directly linked to her frustrating behaviors. Casey loved sweets, books, and cooking, so her rewards in the token economy reflected that as well.

Casey's Reward Chart

	Monday	Tuesday	Wednesday	Thursday	Friday	Saturday	Sunday
Put books away							
Shower without complaining							
Please/ Thank you							
Try a new food							
Practice piano							
Set table							
TOTALS							

If I get 5 points, then I can have 5 extra minutes to play before bedtime.

If I get 10 points, then I can have a small sweet treat (cereal, marshmallow, chocolate chips).

If I get 20 points, then I can take a trip to the ice-cream store.

If I get 35 points, then I can have a turn in the kitchen making something.

If I get 50 points, then I can have a toy or a book from Barnes & Noble.

Quick Tips

- Behavior on the chart must be observable and quantifiable.
- Reward or acknowledgment of the reward must be immediate and consistent.
- Start rewards with the rule of three: one easy task, one occasional task, one stretch task.
- Break up difficult behaviors into smaller, more manageable ones.
- Use age-appropriate rewards and make sure they are meaningful to the child.
- Don't try to work on every behavior or every trouble time of day. Pick the worst and start there.

- Rewards that are earned cannot be taken away under any circumstances.
- The younger the child, the more immediate the rewards need to be.
- Keep it simple, especially at first.
- For a very special reward that will take time to earn, have a meter to show progress.
- When a child already shows internal motivation for a task, don't use an external reward.
- Phase out rewards as the child develops consistency with the behavior or task.
- Pace yourself with prizes. Don't give a big gift for the first success. Build up to it.

How to Praise

→ Be specific about what behavior you liked.

→ Use an excited voice.

→ Be authentic.

→ Praise immediately following the desired behavior.

CHAPTER 10

Consequences

The consequences of an act affect the probability of its occurring again.
                                            —B. F. SKINNER

A CONSEQUENCE IS WHAT happens as a result of an action. As discussed in Chapter 2 with A-B-C (Antecedent-Behavior-Consequence), if these consequences provide a benefit for behavior, we should expect to see more of that behavior. Ignore it! eliminates the benefit of the behavior so that the behavior wanes. However, *inaction* can also curb behavior. When Ignore it! is applied so parents avoid stepping in to muddle natural consequences, it can also improve behavior.

Additionally, consequences can act to deter behaviors. If one is scared of what might happen, one may choose *not* to do an unapproved action. For example, people go to jail when they break the law. This is in an effort to teach others that an action (selling drugs, brandishing a weapon, breaking and entering, stealing) is wrong and will produce unpleasant consequences. If one gets caught cheating on a test, failure is all but inevitable. Showing up late for work will result in less pay. Clear consequences send a well-defined message: don't do it because it isn't worth it.

If I were an Olympian, I'd be scared to death to use even a mildly questionable substance. Imagine training for an entire life to compete in a tournament that comes around only once every four years . . . only to blow it by being caught cheating. The International Olympic Committee (IOC) has created a strict drug-testing policy considered to be the gold standard in sports. The top five athletes in all medal events are automatically tested. Others are tested randomly. Athletes can be tested before or after an event and can be tested repeatedly. Blood and urine samples are taken and stored for eight years in case improved testing procedures are developed. Furthermore, the testing is performed at such a high level that drug use can be detected up to six months back.

When an athlete tests positive, the consequences are enormous. If one gets lucky, he is only stripped of a medal. At worst, he faces the public humiliation of a lifetime ban. The IOC lays out clear expectations for behavior and formidable predictable penalties. The consequences for behavior are known before the possibility of cheating could exist, thereby preventing a lot of unwanted behavior (doping). Imagine if these policies didn't exist. Absolutely everyone would cheat, and the outcomes of the Olympics would be meaningless.

Unlike the IOC, parents routinely forget to set clear expectations for behavior. After an infraction, they fail to impose logical consequences for the actions. Consequences, if executed correctly, can help curb behavior. While Ignore it! allows parents to stop reinforcing undesirable behaviors, consequences are needed as a tool when children don't listen or misbehave in ways that cannot be ignored.

Behaviors that cannot be ignored were discussed in Chapter 3. Here are the highlights as they relate to imposing consequences: Parents cannot ignore sneaky behaviors such as taking money or food or a credit card from parents. They can't ignore children willfully disobeying rules such as using a cell phone after stated hours or arriving late for curfew. Dangerous behavior such as driving without a license or operating machinery sans requisite training should also not be ignored. Last, anything a child does that is illegal (drinking, smoking, vandalism) must be addressed. All of these behaviors require parents to respond to the actions with consequences.

There is just one more category of behavior that shouldn't be ignored that we didn't discuss in Chapter 3. Mom asks Junior to empty the dishwasher, but he doesn't. Dad tells his sweet, darling daughter to turn off the television, but she doesn't make a move. It's time to leave the house to get to school on time and little Jimmy won't put his shoes on after Mom has asked twice. Parents should *not* ignore children ignoring their requests. Parents need to enforce consequences to children's actions when they are against a parent's rules or requests. Ignore it! requires parents to ignore inappropriate behavior or attention-seeking behaviors. Willful disobedience does not fall into this category.

Some parents may worry that if they practice Ignore it!, they will be teaching their children to ignore them. Why would it be okay for Mom and Dad to ignore Junior's constant negotiating but Junior isn't allowed to ignore his parents' pesky requests? Because parents and children are not equals. Families aren't democracies. Parents do have different privileges from children. Parents can drink and eat what they like; children cannot. Parents have a late bedtime; children do not. Furthermore, parents are ignoring only annoying and attention-seeking behavior. If children want to ignore those same behaviors in their parents, that's probably fine. It might even improve relationships. Just as I would ask parents to respect the rules set forth by a teen for, let's say, privacy, I expect children to respect the stated rules and expectations of the parents.

Parental Pitfalls with Consequences

There are three major mistakes parents make with respect to consequences:

- Failing to impose them
- Imposing them too frequently
- Setting them too high or low

These mistakes all take away from the effectiveness of consequences.

Parenting used to primarily concern providing love, some structure, and meeting the basic needs of children. That was pretty much it. As a child, if I forgot my flute at home, no one was going to bring it to me before band practice (feel free to call my mother on this one). If I got a bad grade on a test, neither of my parents would have considered debating the issue with my teacher. In fact, they probably didn't even know about it. Times were different. Kids were often implored to fend for themselves.

Alas, parenting has changed. Nowadays, mothers and fathers work hard to prevent children from experiencing any kind of discomfort. And—wrongheadedly—consequences are often seen as discomfort. Parents are protective by nature, but some consistently intervene to help children avoid any kind of failure. This is an enormous mistake. Children learn from their experiences, but when parents repeatedly butt in on each and every troubling matter, they set children up to have difficulty navigating the real world.

Failing to allow for consequences for behavior we would like to see changed is akin to promoting it. A teen who sneaks out his bedroom window after dark but experiences no punishment is likely to think that behavior is okay with his folks. What of the child who asks for an extra cookie, is told no, but takes one anyway? Here's the lesson she learns: "To heck with rules, to heck with laws. This is my world, and when I want a chocolate chip cookie, I'm taking it. Who is going to stop me?"

Some parents impose consequences with reckless abandon. They are authoritative in nature and expect an extraordinary level of compliance. Either that or they have children who exhibit a great deal of undesirable behavior. (This can be due to a developmental diagnosis or the presence of lots of rewards for unwanted behavior as discussed throughout this book). When parents take away privilege after privilege, eventually children feel there is nothing left to lose. There is no way to discipline a child who just doesn't care anymore.

Take away a teen's phone, computer, *and* video game at once and the child might lose all motivation to improve behavior. This is the danger of using consequence too frequently or too harshly. Often, parents who are punishing constantly are also forgetting to reward children for their positive behavior. That's a double whammy.

The last mistake made by parents is putting forth a consequence that has no impact. If mothers and fathers take something away from the child that has zero emotional value, the child will not feel the impact. Louise, for example, is a little girl who used to love her sticker book. It was her prized possession. But she kind of gave it up six months back. Stickers, she discovered, just stick. They don't dance or sing or smell like flowers or explode into bits. Yawn.

So now she's into Pokémon. One day, after Louise failed to put her toys away, her parents decide to take away the sticker book. They even make a big production about it—sit Louise down, explain to her what she did wrong. "Because of this," her father says, "we are taking away . . . your sticker book!" Well, Louise can barely suppress a smile. She hasn't opened the thing in forever. Therefore, the consequence will have no effect on curbing future behavior.

The purpose of using a consequence is to immediately stop the behavior. But a second (and almost more important) purpose is for the child to remember the consequence so she doesn't make the same mistake again. When parents penalize behavior appropriately, the maximum benefit is achieved.

Natural Consequences and Ignore It!

Outcomes to behavior that are not orchestrated by parents are called natural consequences. Children learn from unpleasant moments. We all do. Have you ever accidentally grabbed a hot pan from the stove with your bare hand? If you have, two things likely happened: 1. Your skin was burned. 2. From that moment on you knew to wear an oven mitt before touching a hot object. You learned an important lesson through an unpleasant experience. Of course, I am not suggesting we let children get burned. But we should allow them to discover that sometimes something unpleasant happens in the aftermath of an action.

If you never fall off a bike, you don't develop the balance to *not* fall off a bike. If you never trip over untied laces, you fail to see the importance in tying them. These sorts of lessons—painful, uncomfortable, requisite—help children decide to do it all differently next time. Nothing modifies a child's behavior more efficiently than natural consequences.

Here are some classic examples of children receiving natural consequences:

- A child forgets his homework and receives a zero for the assignment.
- A teen leaves the house without a coat in the middle of winter. When the sun sets, he freezes his rear off.
- A middle schooler decides to dye her hair blue without permission. She ends up with locks the color of seaweed. She hates it, classmates nickname her "Squid Girl," and she cries herself to sleep.
- A child protests at dinner because she says she hates meat sauce. This is nonsense—she's eaten meat sauce a solid 422 times in her life. But fine, no dinner. Mom says she will not have anything until breakfast. The child goes to bed hungry, and the rumbling of an empty stomach keeps her up at night.

These natural consequences are painful and unpleasant and they will unquestionably inform future decisions made by these kids.

Here's the trouble: because parents intervene prematurely, children often miss the unpleasantness of their actions. Mom and Dad swoop in to rescue the day. Sometimes parents even feel proud of all they do to help their offspring avoid missteps. And, to be clear, I understand the impulse. We all want to do a good job parenting. But without realizing it, parents who pre-empt the lightbulb moment remove the learning opportunity for children. We have to let our kids fall, scrape, cut, fail, underachieve. It's not fun, but it's vital.

Worst of all, parents are actually positively reinforcing the behavior they would like to eliminate. And we know that behavior that is reinforced will surely continue.

If you are dropping off your son's forgotten lunch, books, homework, equipment, etc., please <u>TURN AROUND</u> and exit the building.

Your son will learn to <u>problem-solve</u> in your absence.

The Catholic High School for Boys in Little Rock, Arkansas, Sign to Parents

In an effort to curb parental interruption of a teachable moment involving natural consequences, the Catholic High School for Boys in Little Rock, Arkansas, posted a sign on the front door of the school. It reads, *If you are dropping off your son's forgotten lunch, books, homework, equipment, etc., please TURN AROUND and exit the building. Your son will learn to problem-solve in your absence.* The idea is for children to experience life the so-called "hard way" by feeling their mistakes. In other words, natural consequences teach children to be more responsible for their work and belongings.

Here are the same scenarios I mentioned above—but *without* the natural consequences.

- A child forgets his homework but calls Mom to bring it before seventh period. She rushes to school and the child submits the assignment on time.

- A teen leaves the house without a jacket in the middle of winter. When the thermometer hits seventeen degrees, the teen calls home and asks his babysitter if she could drop off a coat at his friend's house. Well, of course she can. The teen never feels cold.

- A middle schooler decides to dye her hair blue without permission. She ends up with locks the color of seaweed. She hates it and runs crying to her parents. They are appalled and dash her off to the nearest hair salon to have it dyed back. They even pay the $60. All is fixed by the time the girl heads to school on Monday.

- A child protests at dinner because she says she hates pasta with meat sauce (even though she has eaten it 422 times). She decides not to have dinner. But when she whines and moans later on, her folks decide that a small snack might be appropriate. The child eats an apple and a piece of cheese. She goes to bed with a full stomach, and she didn't have to eat the pasta.

The only thing a child learns from his parents rushing

forgotten homework to school is that his missteps matter little. Should he be more mindful about where he places his completed assignment? Meh—why? Mom's there. And do you think the girl who refused dinner learned the consequences of skipping a meal? Nope. She has been officially taught that meals are optional. She can skip less enjoyable foods and expect room-service hours later.

These are not the messages parents seek to be conveyed. What they want is for their kids to be responsible, to eat at meals, and to listen to instructions. But it doesn't work this way. Children need to learn a few lessons on their own. We don't do children any favors by shielding them from real-life consequences. Someday, they will have to live in the real world. They will have to show up on time to a big work meeting, with all of the important documents in tow. Unless you're planning on a late-in-life career as your adult child's twenty-four-hour gopher, now is the time to stop enabling this behavior.

Children don't trust grown-ups to know how everything will work out. They often believe they know more than the adults in their lives. The general belief is that parents are clueless. When I recently tried to tell my twelve-year-old daughter what would happen if she didn't brush her hair, she laughed me off. Then, a week later, when the hairstylist told her she needed to chop off her hair because dreadlocks had formed, she got the message. I'd told her what would happen. She didn't listen because I'm a dumb adult who doesn't know anything. But I can tell you that after losing big chunks of hair, she is pretty committed to brushing now. And the best part about the natural consequence is that I don't have to nag her to brush anymore. She has internalized that need.

||||||||||||||||||||||||||||||||||||||||||||||||||||||||||||||||||||||||||||||||||||||

Natural consequence: An outcome to an action that is unplanned

||||||||||||||||||||||||||||||||||||||||||||||||||||||||||||||||||||||||||||||||||||||

If parents let children deal with their mistakes, invaluable lessons are learned. The tricky part is allowing children to have the "oh, crap" moment. Resist the strong urge to save the day. By using Ignore it!, parents can learn to tolerate the barrage of begging, whining, and negotiating that surely follows when one says, "No, I won't drive you to school because you missed the bus. You will have to walk," or when your child insists that you are the meanest parent in town because you refuse to offer an alternative for dinner. Hang tough and Ignore it! all. By using Ignore it!, parents can kill two birds with one stone. They will not reinforce the behavior (not brushing hair) that resulted in a natural consequence (hair being cut off). Additionally, they will not be reinforcing the response behavior (whining, arguing, etc.).

Scenario	What NOT to Do	Natural Consequence
Child misbehaves at basketball practice.	Talk to the coach to mediate.	Coach doesn't start child in game.
Child does not put toys away.	Put toy away.	Younger sibling messes game up or dog chews toy.
Child forgets to plug in cell phone.	Plug it in for the child.	Cell phone is dead the next day.
Child forgets to turn off electronic game.	Turn it off.	Batteries are dead in the morning; child can't play toy.
Child gets a bad grade on assignment.	Call teacher to argue for additional points.	Child doesn't make honor roll or get into advanced class.
Child refuses food offered at meal.	Make substitutions or provide snacks before next meal.	Hunger

Scenario	What NOT to Do	Natural Consequence
Child can't find all pieces of Tae Kwon Do uniform.	Search the house for missing item.	Child cannot take belt test and must wait another week.
Child treats a belonging poorly.	Iron or repair item.	Child can't wear or use belonging because of abuse.
Child forgets gym uniform at home.	Bring uniform to child.	Child has to pick up garbage around the school instead of participating in gym class. Child is humiliated.
Child wants to wear ridiculous outfit that's either not weather appropriate, doesn't match, or doesn't fit occasion.	Bring an extra outfit in the car.	Child feels embarrassed, too hot, too cold, or uncomfortable.
Child leaves clothes on floor and doesn't put in laundry basket.	Pick up dirty clothes off of floor and wash them.	Favorite shirt isn't washed in time for school picture.
Child is told not to use toy in unintended way. Child continues to use toy inappropriately.	Continue to tell child not to use toy in that manner. Buy a new toy when it breaks.	Toy breaks and child can't use it.
Child didn't finish assignment on time for school.	Let child stay home from school to finish work.	Grade gets marked down for lateness.
Child doesn't take care in putting away game pieces.	Put pieces away for child.	Important game piece is missing next time child wants to play.
Child keeps room messy and disorganized.	Clean room for child. Find missing items lost in room.	Precious items break or are misplaced.
Child doesn't empty swim bag after practice.	Empty bag for child.	Suit is still wet and dirty two days later, when it needs to be worn for tournament.
Child is slow to move in morning and missed bus.	Drive child to school.	Child walks with heavy backpack or has to pay for a taxi with own money.

There are three situations where natural consequences cannot be used.

1. If the consequence would not be felt by the child immediately, this usually breaks the connection between the action and outcome. Therefore, the child may not learn a lesson from the potential discomfort of an action.

2. Natural consequences cannot be used when the outcome is dangerous. For example, we can't just allow kids to play in the street and risk getting hit by a car or allow them to stick their hands into a fire. Parents need to take precautions so that children are safe from danger.

3. When others might be hurt by the child's behavior, parents should intervene. If a child decides to take scissors and cuts his little sister's hair off, who feels the natural consequence? The little sister, not the hair cutter. Therefore, parents will need to use other kinds of consequences to show the boy he cannot cut hair.

Characteristics of Useful Consequences

There are four characteristics of consequences that allow the parents to help the child learn what behavior is undesirable. These characteristics are:

- Logical
- Related

- Reasonable
- Meaningful

When parents cannot allow natural consequences to be felt by the child, they should impose logical ones for unwanted behavior. *Logical* consequences are responses to behavior that are set forth by the parent. They are logical because the consequences aren't random, but instead are picked out for a teaching purpose. Logical consequences are meant to be a substitute for natural consequences in that they provide discomfort for the child as a learning tool.

For example, if a child uses her iPad when she is told she shouldn't, parents can impose a consequence of less iPad time the following day. The penalty for misbehavior is directly related to the cause of the penalty. If a child is caught stealing extra donuts after being told to take only one, the parents can enforce a "no sweets" rule for the next few days. The child will sorely miss dessert, especially when everyone else is having it. This will help the child remember not to take extra sweets next time she is tempted. When imposing a logical consequence, the key is to pick something that will aid in the child's learning.

Consequences should be directly *related* to the behavior. Often, parents penalize the child with a specific sentence. They always do the same thing. Some take away video games while others limit cell phone and computer use. Some parents focus on removing dessert while others send kids to their rooms. These are fairly decent consequences. The issue is that when parents rely on a particular consequence without regard to the specific behavior, they are only imposing a punishment.

Punishment is different from a consequence in a small but significant way. A punishment is retribution, whereas a consequence is a teaching opportunity. If consequences aren't directly related to the behavior, the parent may be punishing the child. Punishment isn't so effective as targeted consequences. When the consequence is related to the behavior, it helps children learn what not to do.

|||||||||||||||||||||||||||||||||||||||||||||||||||||||||||||||||||||||||||||||||||||||||||||||||||||||||||||||||

A punishment is retribution, whereas a consequence is a teaching opportunity.

|||||||||||||||||||||||||||||||||||||||||||||||||||||||||||||||||||||||||||||||||||||||||||||||||||||||||||||||||

Consequences must be *reasonable* to be effective. By "reasonable," I mean neither too stringent nor too lenient. They must reflect the level of the behavior. If a child misplaces a parent's favorite lipstick, the parent shouldn't ban makeup for a year. It might be more reasonable to say the child cannot use Mom's makeup for a week.

On the other hand, if a teen sneaks out of the house and takes the brand-new car around the neighborhood, it isn't enough of a consequence to forbid driving for a day. In order for a consequence to be meaningful, it has to be felt uncomfortably by the child. Make sure the level of consequence matches the severity of the behavior.

One of the most important characteristics of an effective consequence is that it *must* be *meaningful* for the child. Imagine a teen asks on Monday to invite a friend to sleep over Friday night. The kid's room looks like a bomb went off, so you insist that the friend can sleep over only if the room is cleaned. But when Friday rolls around, the teen feels kind of unmotivated and a little tired. He could do without the sleepover, so he decides not to clean his room. When Mom returns form work on Friday to see the room is still a mess, she says, "As a consequence of you not cleaning your room, you cannot have a sleepover tonight." The boy balks and looks peeved—but really he isn't. He already made plans to play video games online with his friend. Mom's consequence is ineffective, so it's almost like not having one.

A similar example is taking away dessert as a consequence. For someone like my daughter, that is a very meaningful consequence. She loves dessert. But if my sister did the same for my nephew, he would shrug his shoulders and say, "Fine." He doesn't have a sweet tooth. My sister would need to find a more meaningful consequence for her son.

Here's one more good example: Sixteen-year-old Michael obsesses about his online avatar in his favorite virtual reality game. He spends hours playing online with his virtual friends. One day he forgets to lug the trash out on time because he was too busy in his cyber world. Mom and Dad decide to take the game away until the next trash day. You better believe this was a meaningful consequence for Michael. And, I'd add, quite a related one, too. Perfect choice. In order for kids to feel the absence of a privilege or property, they have to assign considerable meaning to it.

Four Types of Consequence

Loss of Privilege	Loss of Item	Penalty	Task
Dessert	Cell phone	Time-out	Chores of any kind
Use of certain toys	Computer	Fine	Babysitting
Video games	Favorite toy	Loss of allowance	Driving
Computer time	Book	Cancel outing	Running errands
Deleting apps		Missing sports game	Cleaning
Reading before bed			Making meal
Playtime			Emptying dishwasher
No dates with friends			

Clear Expectations

Remember how I said earlier that were I an Olympian I'd be terrified to use any type of banned substance for fear of being disqualified? I feel that way because the International Olympic Committee lays out crystal-clear expectations for athletes. Well, mothers and fathers need to do the same for their children. Oftentimes parents forget to convey their expectations for behavior. Without a road map for how to behave, children often don't act as a parent expects. This leads to frustration on the part of parents and children. Realistic and clear expectations allow children to feel in control of managing the requirements of their life. It also allows parents to back off and stop nagging.

If parents miss the opportunity to communicate expectations to the child, it sets the youngster up for failure. Children who know the rules are certainly more likely to follow them. They might not instinctively know how to behave in a restaurant or church. They might struggle with knowing how loudly to speak at a park versus inside the waiting room of a doctor's office. They might not grasp that it is inconsiderate to color with a Sharpie on the walls of someone's newly painted kitchen. It is up to parents to explain the rules to their children.

In any given situation, make sure your child knows what's expected. Before heading into the supermarket, take a moment to remind the kids that running around the store is unacceptable, and they cannot open boxes of cereal until they arrive home. Outside of the restaurant, tell the kids that you expect them to stay seated in their chairs for the entire meal. If you are meeting an old college friend who has children, remind your child to be polite even if she isn't thrilled about the afternoon plans.

Part of communicating clear expectations is explaining what will happen if the child doesn't meet the expectations. Parents should tell children in very clear terms:

1. Here is my expectation.
2. If you don't meet the expectation, here is what will happen. (If appropriate, write the expectation down in full view of the child.)

Here's how it works: The Willises were having trouble with Malcolm, their fourteen-year-old son. He would borrow their belongings without asking. This was a problem because he frequently broke or misplaced his parents' belongings. Mr. Willis said to Malcolm, "I expect you to ask to borrow any of my clothing, headphones, or electronics before taking them. If I find that you have disobeyed this rule, you will not be allowed to borrow anything for the next week." Mr. Willis then wrote down this expectation on several Post-it notes and put them in his closet as a reminder for Malcolm. This was perfectly done— Mr. Willis made clear the expectation and what would happen should Malcolm misbehave. This proposed consequence was an excellent choice for Malcolm because it was related, logical, and meaningful. Malcolm had never gone a day without asking to borrow something. Mr. Willis knew if he misbehaved after hearing the expectations, the consequence would be difficult for Malcolm.

After a child knows what is expected and that child chooses to misbehave, then the parent should begin to either Ignore it! or apply an appropriate consequence. Make sure the expectations are realistic, in line with the child's capabilities, and clearly communicated.

Important Points to Remember

- There are three major mistakes parents make with respect to consequences: failing to impose them, imposing them too frequently, and setting them too low or too high.
- Natural consequences obviate the need to nag.
- Intervening to "help" allows children to miss the unpleasantness of their actions.
- Effective consequences are logical related to the behavior, reasonable, and meaningful for the child.

CHAPTER 11

Prevention

An ounce of prevention is worth a pound of cure.

—Benjamin Franklin

THE OTHER DAY at the supermarket, I was squeezing plums when I came upon a terrible-yet-all-too-common scene. There was a mother trying to accomplish a full shop while accompanied by her twin daughters. The girls looked to be, oh, two or three, and both were crying for some Goldfish crackers.

Mom was dressed in workout gear, wearing a T-shirt with the name of a popular local exercise program on it. Mom had yet to pay for the Goldfish, so she calmly explained that eating would have to wait. The girls did not want to hear it. Before long, both children were putting on a storewide screaming exhibition that would have made Andrea Bocelli proud. I could see Mom turning increasingly frazzled. She held one child to her hip as the other sat in the cart. Both were yelling, hollering, begging, barking. By the time Mom reached the checkout, the twin she was holding had begun to punch her stomach. The other still screamed. Mom had the checkout clerk scan the

Goldfish as quickly as possible, then she ripped the bag open for the girls.

Mom paid and dashed out of the store.

So, while what I'm about to say is a little bit of an assumption, it's one that comes via a lifetime of experience. A scene like this is sometimes unavoidable. But frequently it unfolds as a result of poor planning. The incident occurred at noon, which for most toddlers is either lunchtime or in the range of nap time. It is the absolute worst hour to try to food shop. Mom also looked like she had taken the girls to her exercise class before coming to the market.

Look, I get it. I'm not passing judgement. Not a parent around hasn't had that exact same scenario happen. Raising children is a bear. You need a release. Oftentimes, it's exercise. I know what it's like to feel so exhausted and deprived that even though the timing isn't perfect one *needs* to do that exercise class. However, part of parenting is being realistic, and in this case it looks like Mom tried to cram too much into a morning. By the time they entered the store, the girls were tired and hungry. Truthfully, Mom probably was, too. A bit of better planning could have changed that entire experience for all three involved.

Mom had a few options she could have considered. She could have made a choice between food shopping and the exercise class. True, that night's dinner may well have been scrambled eggs or spaghetti or pizza delivery, but, well, so what? The world doesn't stop spinning with a less-than-ideal meal every now and then. Alternatively, Mom could have gone to a quick convenience store for a few small items after class and done a bigger shop the following morning. Last, she could have planned ahead and given the girls peanut butter–and-jelly sandwiches or bags of cut-up veggies in the supermarket. She could have had a few special toys in her bag for them after they were finished.

Now, whenever someone tries to help an overly taxed (and exhausted) parent learn master planning, it can be an uphill battle. It seems that nothing is negotiable. You know how it is—the kids have to take their ballet and Gymboree. Mom and Dad need to exercise, too. Grandma wants to meet for dinner but not until seven thirty on a school night. The schedule is often "go, go, go." But while the parents are accomplishing everything on their must-do list, they aren't enjoying most of it.

Ignore it! is a powerful tool aimed at minimizing unwanted behavior. However, sometimes there are other ways to prevent meltdowns, tantrums, and other disagreeable behavior by improving preparation. This chapter is devoted to helping parents strengthen their planning.

Timing

In parenting, timing is everything. For example, I am not a very nice person when I'm hungry. My blood sugar goes low, and I can't think or talk or do much of anything until I eat. Children are often the same way. The difference between a child and me is that I can say to my husband, "I have to get something to eat or I'm going to lose it." Indeed, I have uttered this exact sentence a solid five thousand times. It means, in no ambiguous terms, I *need* to eat.

Children, however, lack this ability. They don't give a warning. They don't throw you a heads-up. They don't say, "Um, Dad, just to be clear . . ." Nope. They just lose it. I've seen it happen with teens as often as toddlers. While the presentation may appear different, the problem is the same. Some people just can't handle hunger. For kids, parents have to plan ahead to make sure children eat within a reasonable time frame. This one tip can help them avoid a plethora of bad moments.

I also recommend keeping a bunch of healthy snacks in the car or your bag for last-minute delays. This may seem obvious, but it is often forgotten. Also, sometimes parents are rushing out the door and they simply don't have time to prepare something. Alternatively, they did have snacks but they ran out the other day. Whatever the reason, a bit of extra organization can be helpful. I also recommend putting a sticky note on the front or garage door to remind you to grab snacks. And as I said, kids young and old need snacks.

One quick note about snacks. Sometimes kids are snacking too much or at the wrong times. Studies show that snacking has increased dramatically over the last forty years. Now snacking accounts for 27 percent of children's daily calorie count. Most kids are having three meals *and* three snacks a day. This is grazing behavior and often leads to difficult behavior at meals. I have observed many a household where kids are having snack after snack, then they refuse dinner. Parents are frustrated at meals and want their children to eat. A battle of wills at the table ensues.

However, snacks are acting as substitute meals. Cutting back snacks and providing them only at strategic times of the day will help avoid mealtime dramas. Also, when children don't eat lunch because of protests, they will naturally be hungry shortly after mealtime. Parents sometimes make the mistake of giving snacks at that time. But, again, this reinforces that meals aren't essential. Planning meals and snacks for the day can help parents avoid some of these pitfalls.

While parents should have some flexibility in their lives, I have found that the vast majority of kids thrive on a schedule. This means that bedtime generally stays the same. Lunch and dinner are at a consistent time every day. And naps are respected without regular interruption or shifting. Why is the schedule so important? Well, because kids have needs. If those needs aren't met promptly, things can turn ugly. Overtired children aren't pleasant. Chronically overtired children are unbearable. Making sure children receive the right amount of sleep for their age is vital (see the "How Much Sleep Does Your Child Need?" chart on p. 176). But all too often, life gets in the way. There's a neighborhood gathering on Friday night, so the kids are up a bit late. No big deal.

Then Saturday night, Grandma is having an anniversary party. Again, the children are up way past their bedtime. On Sunday evening, the church is organizing a movie night. The kids are begging to go, even though they wouldn't be home until after nine thirty. Monday night is the awards banquet for the oldest child, so again another late night. Meanwhile, with each consecutive late night, behavior is getting a little bit worse. They have less ability to cope with life. There are more outbursts and fights. Harsher words are spoken. There is more dawdling, followed by frustrated rushing. Lack of sleep takes its toll and is rarely recognized as the culprit for some of the behavior. By all means, live life. Go out for dinner, but not when the meal will push the kids' limits. Respect sleep because if you don't you will pay for that night out with rough behavior. In the case of teenagers, make certain they aren't having back-to-back sleepovers or night parties. There might be no one crankier than a teen who has been running on fumes for days.

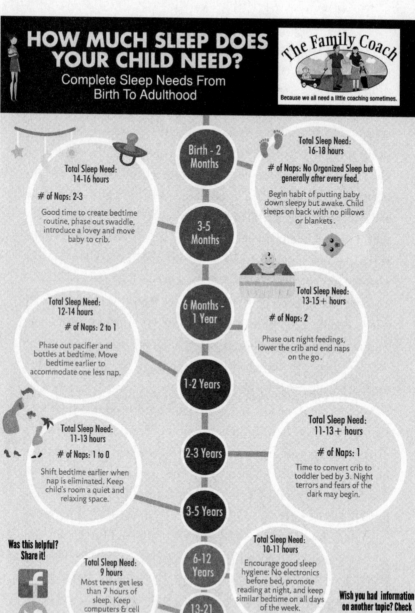

HOW MUCH SLEEP DOES YOUR CHILD NEED?

Complete Sleep Needs From Birth To Adulthood

The Family Coach
Because we all need a little coaching sometimes.

Birth - 2 Months

Total Sleep Need:
16-18 hours

# of Naps: No Organized Sleep but generally after every feed.

Begin habit of putting baby down sleepy but awake. Child sleeps on back with no pillows or blankets.

3-5 Months

Total Sleep Need:
14-16 hours

# of Naps: 2-3

Good time to create bedtime routine, phase out swaddle, introduce a lovey and move baby to crib.

6 Months - 1 Year

Total Sleep Need:
13-15+ hours

# of Naps: 2

Phase out night feedings, lower the crib and end naps on the go.

Total Sleep Need:
12-14 hours

# of Naps: 2 to 1

Phase out pacifier and bottles at bedtime. Move bedtime earlier to accommodate one less nap.

1-2 Years

2-3 Years

Total Sleep Need:
11-13+ hours

# of Naps: 1

Time to convert crib to toddler bed by 3. Night terrors and fears of the dark may begin.

Total Sleep Need:
11-13 hours

# of Naps: 1 to 0

Shift bedtime earlier when nap is eliminated. Keep child's room a quiet and relaxing space.

3-5 Years

6-12 Years

Total Sleep Need:
10-11 hours

Encourage good sleep hygiene: No electronics before bed, promote reading at night, and keep similar bedtime on all days of the week.

13-21 Years

Total Sleep Need:
9 hours

Most teens get less than 7 hours of sleep. Keep computers & cell phones out of bedrooms.

Was this helpful? Share it!

Wish you had information on another topic? Check out our website.

TheFamilyCoach.com

Toy Bag

Generally, I see two extremes in restaurants: kids are either unruly disasters or kids are glued to iPads. Sure, some kids are delightful. I'm not talking about those kids for now. Parents sitting alongside misbehaving kids tend to ignore them, which ruins the meal for all seventy nearby diners and makes the waiter, the busboy, and the maître d' want to strangle your little Thomas.

But the "let's just shove this iPad in front of Junior for the next three hours" approach is equally unwise. Yes, it maintains a high level of silence. But how do children learn to interact with others, or eat properly in a formal setting, or appreciate a meal, when they're busy watching *Alvin and the Chipmunks: The Road Chip*? Children don't merely show up to the Four Seasons for high tea knowing how to behave. It's the quick meals at Panera or Pizza Hut that prime children to tolerate (and, really, enjoy and embrace) longer meals. Recently, I met a friend for lunch at Olive Garden (gotta admit, the salad and breadsticks are the best). I was horrified to see each table equipped with its very own game-packed iPad. Hey, thanks, Olive Garden! Just when my children were accepting restaurants as a place to sit and engage, you give them screens.

Now parents have an additional hurdle to conquer. Of course the kids will beg and plead to play some games. And when parents are hungry and a bit overwhelmed themselves, they are prone to give in. But the problem with the iPad at dinner is children aren't having conversations with parents. They aren't interacting with waitstaff or using table manners. And they aren't building skills or relationships, either. Fast-forward a few years and parents will be dealing with sulky teens who won't even glance toward a waiter or a parent in a restaurant, let alone talk to them about what is happening in life. While it is never too late to make a change, it certainly is a lot easier when the patterns are set much earlier.

Enter . . . the toy bag. My older sister taught me the art of the toy bag when her children were little. The bag is simply a stash of activities that help keep kids happy, occupied, and engaged while waiting for food in a restaurant or when there is an unexpected delay. Perfect items for the bag include crayons and markers for coloring, card games of any kind, small cars or mini-skateboards, Wikki Stix, magnetic travel games, and figurines (Playmobil, dinosaurs, animals, Disney princesses, Polly Pockets, Shopkins). The games and toys in the bag should be different from the ones at home. This helps keep them fresh and exciting. As kids' interests change, you can update the bag.

I have to say I am addicted to buying items for the toy bag. Even though my daughter is nearly thirteen, she still asks, "What's in your bag?" Anything small that can fit in my pocketbook is a weakness for me. Some family favorites are Uno, Sushi Go!, and Crazy Faces. I believe my family might hold the record for the greatest number of Uno games played. It's a game that works for young children as well as it does for grandparents. Fun for the whole family, quick, easy to carry, and it never gets old. We even have a waterproof deck for the beach bag. The best places to shop for toy bag items are Target, Lakeshore Learning or Learning Express, a museum gift shop, or bookshops like Barnes & Noble. Think small, light, quick, and easy cleanup.

Parents don't merely have to rely on the toy bag. There are lots of word games that can also be played to kill the time while waiting somewhere. Play geography, twenty questions, trivia, or have a spelling bee. Take the Sweet'n Low packets and have a contest to build a Queen Elizabeth–worthy sugar castle. Use the napkins and make shapes and animals. Or create mini-forts with jelly packs at the diner. The bottom line: engage. It will improve behavior tremendously and build relationships and skills that will benefit the child and the family.

Exercise

Some children can sit for days reading, playing with small toys, or coloring. Others need much more action. I remember when my neighbor brought home a puppy (yes, I am about to make an analogy between children and dogs again). They named their pup "Mookie" in honor of legendary New York Mets center fielder Mookie Wilson. Much like all puppies, ol' Mook was trouble. He chewed and shredded everything. He constantly nudged people to be rubbed. That dog was adorable but annoying.

One day, however, my neighbor took Mookie out for a marathon-esque walk with a friend. They roamed street after street after street, and upon returning home the dog collapsed to the floor in a heap of exhaustion. For the rest of the afternoon, he slept. After that day, she never missed a long walk with Mookie. And his behavior remained forever delightful.

Many children are just like Mookie. They either burn off a good deal of energy, or they struggle to control behavior.

Studies show that in the aftermath of exercise, thinking skills, self-control, memory, and school performance all improve. And these effects have been shown to be equally true for kids with attention deficit disorder (ADD) or without any diagnosis.

So how much exercise do children need to reap those benefits? In many cases, as little as twenty minutes. If you have a high-energy child (or one who has been diagnosed with ADD/ADHD), I implore you to up their physical activity intake. Sometimes parents want children to come home from school and get right to homework because it can take the child *forever* to get it done. I usually recommend parents take a different tack. Spending thirty minutes having a catch in the front yard or in the park after school can help the child complete homework in shorter time with more focus and fewer interventions from Mom and Dad. If children are doing soccer followed by football all afternoon, the effects might be the opposite. Find the balance for your children so they get a chance to be kids and let off some energy, but not so much that they are exhausted.

Praise

Take a moment and think about how many times you admonished or said no to your child today. How about yesterday? Now think about how many times you praised or gave a thumbs-up or a high five. Most parents provide far more negative attention and reprimands than they do kind words. But those kind words go a long way in improving behavior. Praise has been hotly debated in recent years. First parents were told to praise. Then the word on the street was to hang back on the praise. Kids were scoring too much of a good thing.

Here's the deal. Praise is still pretty important for children. As discussed in Chapter 9, praise is a social reinforcer. It allows children to receive positive attention for a good behavior. Behaviors that are reinforced are more likely to occur. Furthermore, praising one behavior may have a larger effect on other behaviors. For example, one study showed that children whose parents praised them at an early age for their good manners grew to have better social skills.

Have you ever worked really hard on a task at the job, only to have no one even notice? Imagine how unmotivated you would be next time there was an opportunity to go above and beyond. Seems obvious. But the benefits of praise depend greatly on what and how you praise.

Even if it isn't on your reward chart, make a point to acknowledge good deeds and behavior when you see them. Here's how to do it: Don't just say, "Good job." Be specific. What are you praising? Also, focus on praising characteristics that are within your child's ability to modify. For example, praising beauty or innate intelligence ("You are so smart.") isn't superhelpful. However, praising hard work, focus, penmanship, sportsmanship, teamwork, or cleanliness *is* effective in promoting future good behavior. Remember, it's better to praise a child who exerted a significant effort but only obtained a B on a book report than a child who barely tried but snagged the A.

Empty or insincere compliments not only don't have a positive effect on behavior, they often worsen it. Children could write off your words as dishonest. So find something to praise and mean it. If you struggle in this area, keep at it. It's important.

Think about what doesn't come easily for your child. That's what you should be looking at to praise. A child who is typically anxious in social situations but introduces herself to a new girl deserves praise. A boy who hates to read but meets his reading goal at school deserves a nod. The kid who shoots basketballs all week in the driveway and finally lands a free throw in the game should be acknowledged for his hard work.

One last note about praise: make it specific to an individual child's effort and ability. Don't compare one kid to another. Something that comes easily to one child may not warrant recognition. But the child who struggles to make even the smallest improvement might benefit from notice of his effort.

Relationships

Kids who feel loved and supported are much more likely to want to listen and please their parents with good behavior. A child who spends quality time with a parent playing ball or planting a garden or making a gingerbread house is putting money in the bank. In this case, the bank is the relationship between the child and parent. When life turns stressful and behavior deteriorates, it's the underlying relationship that helps parents and children pull through without major damage. That rapport is what will motivate a child to do what is asked of her. Building a positive relationship, especially after there has been long-term strain, is absolutely vital to improving behavior.

If your children regularly seek you out to play or to spend

time together, you are probably all set in the relationship department. However, if you are harboring negative feelings toward a particular child, you have some work to do. It is frowned upon for parents to admit that one child is easier than another, or that they prefer time with one child more than the other. But not acknowledging it doesn't make that strain go away. In fact, often it only exacerbates it.

Make sure your children don't feel criticized or forgotten even if they are difficult. These are the kids who need more love and attention—not to be left alone. If you and your child have been in a constant battle or don't seem to see eye to eye, start setting aside time where you can hang out together. Quality time doesn't have to be every day or for long hours on end. Start by identifying ten minutes where you can put cell phones away and do something *the child* enjoys. During that time, don't direct, control, or carp. Should you do an activity that you will probably hate just because your child loves it? Absolutely. Show your child that you are willing to see what her interest is all about.

I had a client who struggled to develop a relationship with a reclusive teen. The boy loved music. He played the electric guitar and desperately wanted to go to see his favorite band in concert. Mom hated loud music and crowds. The idea of spending a few hours stuffed into a hot venue listening to noise was less than enticing for Mom. Well, after some encouragement, Mom agreed to take her son to the concert. I advised her to keep her mouth shut. She wasn't allowed to complain *at all*. She had to stifle negative thoughts, and I urged her to smile and nod often. Even though Mom hated the music, she loved the evening. Seeing her son have the time of his life in his element showed her a side of him she hadn't known existed. She realized how much negativity she'd been sending toward her son and his interests. The evening was a resounding success.

It wasn't easy for Mom to keep her thoughts to herself. In fact, she said it was one of the most difficult parenting tasks she had ever experienced. But the evening had a transformative effect on both mother and child.

Often in the rush of all other parenting responsibilities, building the relationship can get pushed behind providing basic needs. But behavior and the relationship can go hand in hand. So make sure to give your relationship with your child some attention if it has been less of a focus.

Rushing

Parents and children are at their worst when they are running late or rushing from here to there. Parents lose their temper or take shortcuts that send mixed messages. Young children can almost come to a complete halt when they are rushed. Older or disorganized children are more likely to forget an important item when hurrying about. If you can plan ahead to avoid the mad dash to get out the door in the morning or to have homework, dinner, and bath completed in less than forty-five minutes, you will be able to avoid many a meltdown (from you and your children).

I hate making lunches. It's my most despised parenting chore. I hate it because I am not a morning person. Moving quickly to prepare two very different lunches while simultaneously fixing breakfast is my personal torture. Never mind if I forgot to clean the lunch boxes out from the day before, or if there is a last-minute permission slip to sign, or if money is needed for some PTA function. Mornings work much better for my family if I get a bit organized the night before. Sometimes I pack snacks, drinks, and fruits before going to bed. Other times I make sandwiches and have them ready in the refrigerator. I try to have my kids bring their lunch boxes into the kitchen when they arrive home, and we are working on *them* emptying the contents (admittedly, this is a work in progress).

If there is paperwork to do, I get that all handled the night before. I'm certainly not always successful in this effort. But the amount of yelling and dysfunctional behavior from both child and parent are drastically reduced when I take the time to get organized.

The same issue comes up for parents at the end of the day. Whenever I ask clients to tell me the time of day when they are having the most issues with their children, the number one answer is from four to seven p.m. However, some planning here, too, can ease struggles and improve behavior. Use the slow cooker to prepare dinner in advance so you can focus on helping with homework or doing fun activities with the kids. On the weekend, make bigger meals that can be eaten as leftovers on a busy weeknight. Or better yet, make meals ahead and freeze them for easy reheating whenever you don't feel up to cooking.

It's impossible to cover every way parents can prevent unwanted behavior. But I've given some examples of the kinds of planning I typically recommend when working directly with families. I encourage you to use these tips or take time to assess where you might be able to find ways to be more efficient, schedule in better consideration of the kids' sleep and eating needs, or prepare ahead. It's not always possible. But it is certainly worth a try.

Important Points to Remember

- Meals and sleep schedules should be at a consistent time every day to prevent behavioral issues related to sleepiness and hunger.
- Praise is a social reinforcer, allowing children to receive positive attention for a good behavior.
- Praise should be related to characteristics that are within your child's ability to modify.
- Building a positive relationship with your child is vital to improving behavior.

CHAPTER 12

The Impediments to Success—and How to Fix Them

IGNORE IT! IS a simple program. Ignore, Listen, Reengage, and Repair. Nothing complicated, right?

Um, wrong. While the program is simple, the implementation is not. Children are masterminds at working the system to their advantage. They know what buttons to push, and they aren't afraid to push them. Many well-intentioned and motivated parents become derailed when kids, being kids, go off script. Other failings fall squarely on the parents' shoulders. These unintentional missteps also delay improvement or prevent it from being achieved. This chapter will work through some of the common pitfalls that undercut parental success with Ignore it!.

Ignoring but Not Really Ignoring

Ignoring by definition means:

- To disregard
- To pay no attention
- Refusing to take notice *intentionally*

Often parents believe they are ignoring when, in truth, they are doing everything *but*. Here's what I mean: A father is trying to ignore a child who is having a tantrum. But the child tests the limits of Dad's resolve by screaming, "I hate you!" The parent fires back with, "Great! I don't care!" Then he immediately returns to ignoring.

Well, Ignore it! doesn't allow for intermittent ignoring. It has to be consistently applied. Otherwise the benefits of the behavior are maintained and thus reinforced. This means you cannot respond in any way. No grunts or sighs or sucking teeth. Angry faces or signs that you are being affected by the child's behavior must be invisible. Your body language and face have to all convey that you don't even notice the child's behavior. One time, I observed a mother practicing Ignore it! with her teen daughter. While in the ignoring phase, Mom didn't say one word. But her foot never stopped tapping. Her face was draped with a scowl, and her hand was firmly planted on her hip. She was annoyed, and it would have been obvious to anyone of any age speaking any language in any country. That's a big no-no.

Here's another example of the "ignoring but not really ignoring" pitfall. Mom makes pasta with meatballs, as was requested by the son. When the food arrives, the child starts to protest. He says, "I don't like the meatballs like this! Can't I just have a grilled cheese sandwich?" Mom squashes the suggestion with a firm "No!" But the child isn't used to such a definitive response, so he begins to needle Mom. First, he pushes the food away. Mom ignores this easily until the boy begins to play with the food. Mom resists the urge to admonish and continues to Ignore it!.

Now the son flings a meatball at the dog. Mom rushes over to the child and says, "Fine, if you won't eat this, then don't eat!" She walks away in a huff. Her son didn't want to eat the meatballs to begin with, so taking them away is like a reward. (That's negative reinforcement in action.) Furthermore, as a bonus prize, the son got under Mom's skin. She should have ignored all attempts by the child to engage his mom. As soon as the child stopped making a mess of his food, she needed to re-engage him. She could have explained, in a calm voice, "I understand that you chose not to eat the meatballs. But you cannot mess up the kitchen in protest. Here is a towel; please go clean up the dog and the floor where the meatball landed."

The Preemptive Strike

Sometimes parents don't feel they have the time or energy to do Ignore it!. They try to forestall it— but not in a helpful way. Every few seconds, Mom or Dad might say, "You better stop that or I'll [fill in the punishment]." The problem with this is twofold.

First, parents repeatedly threaten with [fill in the punishment], but they know (and the child knows) that punishment will likely never come. It's a completely empty threat. If the parents were really going to go through with the penalty, they would just act, not merely threaten it. The second issue is that, in the process of trying to avoid having to Ignore it!, the parent is providing the very attention that is reinforcing the behavior.

Offense is your best defense. Be proactive in planning or using the other preventative measures discussed in Chapter 11. However, if the child is already exhibiting the behavior you are trying to eliminate, warning that you will soon start to Ignore it! will not work. In fact, it does the opposite. Just Ignore it! and then it will go away.

Let's Speed This Up

Parents are busy people. Even ones who are conscientiously trying to use Ignore it! find themselves in a bind from time to time. They know they have to Ignore it! until the child stops the behavior. But sometimes they reach a point where they are tired of waiting, so they try to hurry the whole process along. In attempting to rush to the reengage phase of Ignore it!, parents make an important mistake.

Here's an example: Michelle was planning an afternoon at the park with some friends. The idea was to wait until the youngest of her three children woke from a nap, then head out. The two older kids, Natasha and Marni, played chess on the kitchen table as they waited for their sister to wake up. Mom told them to start cleaning up because she wanted to be ready to leave. They requested more time. "Not today. We don't have more time," Mom said. "Please clean up now."

Although Marni followed orders, Natasha wasn't going to take no for an answer. She whined. She complained. She whined some more. On and on she went, but Mom used Ignore it!.

Meanwhile, Marni had put the game away by the time the baby stirred. Mom changed the diaper and was ready to go. The problem was Natasha was still having her tantrum. Mom stood quietly waiting for Natasha to settle so she could reengage her. But it was taking forever. Mom lost her patience. So she said, "Calm down, Natasha, so we can go." Mom just told her in so many words that if she didn't calm down they wouldn't be able to leave. Mom continued to try to speed up the Ignore it! process by offering incentives to stop crying and get in the car. Instead of focusing her attention on the other kids, Mom devoted it all to Natasha, again reinforcing the behavior.

In order for Natasha to learn that arguing and hysterics won't help her out, her mom needed to eliminate the benefits. But in her attempt to rush to the finish line, she provided several. Natasha received loads of attention, and she was able to delay departure to the park. If you start to Ignore it!, make sure to fully wait out the behavior before trying to reengage. This is an enormously important point. Because if you ignore the behavior—but then intervene—you ensure that the behavior will not only continue but likely turn worse. Children might get the message that in order for you to intervene they need to be more dramatic or more obnoxious. Don't let that happen by ignoring completely until the behavior vanishes.

Oops, Forgot a Step

Ignore
Listen
Reengage
Repair

There are four steps to Ignore it!. The first three steps are non-negotiable. They must be completed and in the correct order. The last one is still required, but not in all circumstances. Remember **I L**ike **Re**laxed **Re**ading?

Hopefully, the mnemonic helps you remember the steps and the order. But for a variety of reasons, parents sometimes miss a step. For some parents, ignoring is the easy part. They are so frustrated and exhausted from the aggravated behavior that they are thrilled to look the other way. They relish the momentary break from a difficult relationship.

But those are the same parents who tend to skip the reengage stage. Reengaging with a positive attitude helps parent and child put the incident in the past. It helps make sure behavior ends without residual anger. If parents don't show kids they have moved on by reengaging, there is an increased risk of the behavior returning. So even if you have to fake the positive vibe, put on a happy face and get back in there. Don't shortchange yourself if you are putting in the effort to Ignore it!.

Parents can usually easily remember that kids may need to repair a few things after an incident. They reengage positively and then tell the offender to apologize for behavior or clean up a mess made during a tantrum. But very often, parents forget to make a repair for *their* behavior. Parents are human, and they, too, make mistakes. In a moment of anger, some say mean stuff they soon regret. Some turn aggressive when challenged. Some act out in other ways that are equally damaging to a relationship. Acknowledging where you went wrong in an incident with your child can go a long way in moving on and repairing a troubled relationship.

If you have done something that was unkind, inconsiderate,

or inappropriate, apologize. You can model for your child how it's done. Additionally, apologizing normalizes mistakes. They happen to everyone, even parents. Say sorry and mean it.

What Page Are You On?

Parenting is a tricky job. But when two adults have to parent in the same way, it can feel like trying to corral wild monkeys. People who have a child together were not raised in the same household.

They were, in many cases, parented differently and thus may not see eye to eye on best practices. One may feel children should be seen and not heard, while the coparent grew up with folks who valued his youthful input. Another parent who was raised without any extras now wants to give his children what he didn't have. But his coparent feels the kids are being spoiled. While family of origin certainly influences parenting style, it isn't the only factor. Sometimes parents have different ideas of what's best. One parent loves the kids sharing the family bed. The other is ready to kick 'em to the curb if they don't stay in their own rooms. Dad loves dessert and wants it with the kids every night after dinner. Mom worries about a healthy diet. You get the idea. Mediating parenting styles is a common reason I am called in to work with a family. Mom and Dad are *not* on the same page.

So what's the big deal? Well, kids who receive mixed messages often try to work the system. They can become more manipulative and resourceful in obtaining what they want. And parents who aren't in agreement about how to discipline undermine each other's efforts. If Dad is practicing Ignore it!

whenever Junior turns aggressive but Mom can't resist the urge to teach him a lesson, Dad's hard work will be overturned. Mom will be providing the positive reinforcement for the unwanted behavior.

Parents don't have to do every act the same. Some variety is terrific. In my house, my husband more often than not says yes. *Yes to building giant forts in the basement. Yes to pancakes before school even though there isn't much time. Yes to movie night.* I'm more of the organizer and scheduler. I say no a lot more often. *No, you can't stay up two hours past bedtime. No, you can't have a third brownie even though they are delicious. No, you can't take apart your computer.*

But this diversity of approach works just fine. My kids get the best of both worlds. But when it comes to Ignore it!, positive reinforcement, and discipline, we don't diverge. We are on the same page, and our children see a unified front. If there is a disagreement between us about parenting, we do it privately and try to work on a compromise.

Parents do themselves a disservice when they don't work together. Not everyone has a happy marriage or a willing partner. Coparenting after divorce can be a challenge. But do your best to decide on a few behaviors to accompany Ignore it! to improve the effectiveness of the program. It will benefit all members of the family to wipe out undesirable behavior.

What's the Alternative?

Ignore it! has the ability to greatly reduce unwanted problem behaviors. However, it is much more effective when combined with positive reinforcement for alternative behaviors. Children who beg and plead and negotiate should be rewarded for following initial directions without backlash. Children who are messy disasters all over the house should be encouraged when they put away their clothes. Whiners should be rewarded for asking nicely. Cursers should be praised for skipping inappropriate language in favor of more suitable alternatives. Unfortunately, parents can sometimes forget to reward children for alternative behaviors. They are more focused on the negative ones.

Make sure if you are ignoring undesirable behavior that you are *paying attention* to the desirable ones. That's the only way to encourage those behaviors to occur more often.

If the desired alternative behavior has not been strengthened sufficiently with reinforcement, it will become extinct, too.

Intermittent Reinforcement

Let's say you are doing a bang-up job ignoring all negotiating. You successfully ignored all tantrums and excessive complaining. Your child isn't getting away with snubbing dinner or acting out at Grandma's house. You are doing great.

But you get sick or tired or distracted. In that moment, you are checking out at the supermarket. Even though asking for sweets and toys has greatly diminished because of Ignore it!, your child decides to test your resolve. So he asks, "Can I have this pack of gum?" You say, "No. You can't have gum." Then the begging returns and, in a moment of weakness, you give in. Score one for the little guy. You just practiced intermittent reinforcement. Ignoring most occasions of the undesirable behavior but reinforcing a few instances can still be very motivating.

Behavior that has been inconsistently ignored can become resistant to extinction. The inconsistency can come from one parent ignoring behavior but someone else simultaneously reinforcing it. But it can also happen when parents forget to ignore a behavior some of the time. So if you aren't seeing the success you expected, look to see if you or someone else is intermittently reinforcing the wrong behaviors.

Again, as simple as Ignore it! is, it is also complicated. Children are clever. Parents aren't always so present as they need to be. Life can get in the way. But if Ignore it! isn't going as planned, try to evaluate where you might be going wrong. Reread earlier chapters and try again with a better understanding of the process. Sometimes a small change can make a huge difference. Keep at it until you are seeing the results described in this book.

Important Points to Remember

- The most common mistakes that derail Ignore it! are: not really ignoring, trying to avert the bad behavior, rushing to reengage, and caregivers being on different pages.
- Behavior that has been inconsistently ignored and thus intermittently reinforced can become resistant to Ignore it!.
- Pay attention to desirable behaviors and offer reward or those behaviors might unintentionally become extinct.

CHAPTER 13

Evaluation

T HIS CHAPTER IS optional.

I consider this to be such an important point that I am going to say it again.

This chapter is optional.

I know . . . I know. It's sort of weird for me to kick off this section with a declaration that you may not need the contents. Let me explain. Some readers will see and feel the difference Ignore it! can make. They will notice improved behavior immediately. They will feel that time with their children is increasingly enjoyable. And they will be more in control and less stressed with managing daily behavioral problems. Those parents may not need (or even want) to chart behavior to evaluate effectiveness. They can sense that life is better, and that is good enough for them.

For those folks, this chapter is optional.

That will not be the case for other parents. If you are like me, you want to *know* that something works, with data to prove it. I have a hard time taking someone's word for it. Without research, I would be lost. I like to know there is proof (with evidence) that a claim is true or a medicine cures an illness or a therapy improves behavior. As a family coach, it is imperative that I not waste a client's money and time on treatments that may or may not help. Sure, not everyone responds to every intervention. That's all right. But I need to have knowledge, based on research, that tells me there is a good chance that what I am doing will be helpful.

Many parents will rightly want to know—for certain—that Ignore it! worked for them before recommending it to friends and neighbors. Let's say a child has been a classic negotiator for many years. The parents begin Ignore it! and the negotiating falls off. The improvement is obvious. The parents can tell this to be true. But how do they know the change was due to implementing Ignore it!? Maybe there was some environmental alteration that improved behavior. What if at the same time they began Ignore it!, they also decided to make major diet and exercise changes? In this case it is impossible to know if the improvement was due to Ignore it! or the other changes in the child's life. With careful evaluation, we can determine exactly what helped improve the behavior.

There is another important reason to evaluate Ignore it!. If your child is throwing a tantrum at least ten times a day, you may not notice a difference when it becomes six times. Six times may still feel like your child is tantrumming without halt. But six is better than ten. Improvement is improvement. Tracking can help parents see that Ignore it! is indeed working. But the behavior may have been going on for very long or was intermittently reinforced to such an extent that the process will take longer.

For those parents, seeing improvement will give them enough hope to continue with the program. The worst scenario is that behavior is getting better but not fast enough and parents drop the program. This always breaks my heart. Parents are so close, but when they don't see dramatic enough change they give up. Kids' behavior gets worse and parents feel deflated. Evaluation solves this problem.

Evaluation can also help in one more very important way. Sometimes parents report to me that there are days when their children are delightful. They behave and listen without incident. Other days feel like a nightmare, with tantrums, yelling, and annoyances. Charting the behavior over the course of a few weeks can show key patterns that help explain the variability in behavior. Oftentimes children (and parents) struggle with transitioning into the school and workweek. This can mean that Sunday evenings and Mondays tend to be the roughest. For other families, the kids tend to be great during much of the day, but once the late afternoon hits it all falls apart. Knowing when to anticipate the struggles can greatly help.

Tracking Before Ignore It!

Assessing behavior before an intervention is called, in research circles, a baseline. The purpose of the baseline is to better understand an issue before trying to treat it. The baseline helps establish a starting point for future comparison. Doctors use baseline X-rays to see the progression of disease. Researchers use baseline data to see if an intervention had an impact.

Analysis of data can be quite complicated, but it doesn't have to be. A trend can be seen without any expert knowledge or additional training.

There are apps galore for tracking nearly everything. Weight Watchers tracks food intake. Exercise enthusiasts love to track every step. People track sleep, the number of bathroom breaks, how many glasses of water are consumed. Women also track their cycles and fertile times every month. A lot of useful information can be gleaned from the data that can change habits. And the simple act of charting has been found to be a helpful tool even without an intervention. I'll present a few examples to show how tracking has helped families even before they implement Ignore it!.

> **Assessment:** Systematic measurement of an intervention
>
> **Baseline:** Assessment before an intervention

Sixteen-year-old Josh was a boy who had a very distinct pattern to his behavior. Josh's parents were divorced. He spent the weekdays with his mother, Maria, and alternating weekends with his father. Maria complained about Josh's constant yelling and cursing. She had a hard time talking to him about anything without it escalating. Mom tracked Josh's behavior for two consecutive weeks (Figure 1, p. 202). A pattern quickly emerged, and Mom was simultaneously dumbfounded and thrilled. She was delighted to realize that Josh wasn't yelling at her constantly. In general, he was pretty good during the weekdays, except for Wednesdays (I'll come back to this). This precise information (knowing that there were times when she communicated effectively with her son) brought Maria to tears. She had been feeling like a failure, and feared that her relationship with her son was a lost cause. But the data didn't lie. Mother and son were getting along most of the time.

What dumbfounded Maria was the times the eruptions took place. Josh tended to act up on Sundays, Mondays, and Wednesdays. The difficulties he was experiencing on these days were easily explained. Josh struggled during reintegration into his mom's house after being with Dad for the weekend. This is a common phenomenon.

On Wednesdays, Josh's schedule was jam-packed. He came home from school at three forty-five p.m. By four, the SAT tutor would arrive. As soon as tutoring wrapped, he ate a quick snack and ran out the door for water polo practice. He swam from five thirty until seven and was famished afterward. Once home, Maria made dinner while Josh started on his homework. The rest of the evening was spent eating, showering, completing work, and preparing for bed. Interspersed throughout the myriad tasks was an incredible amount of shouting from both Maria and Josh.

Even without using Ignore it!, charting the days and times when the problems occurred helped Maria change Josh's behavior. She realized she needed to plan better. Tutoring on Wednesday, even though it was convenient for the tutor, wasn't a good day for Josh. She decided to move his tutoring to give him a little downtime before water polo. She also began to prepare dinner ahead of time in the Crock-Pot so it would be ready the second Josh returned home from practice. And she often packed an appetizer for the car ride home.

With these relatively slight changes, Wednesdays with Josh

became much more pleasant. Maria used Ignore it! to handle any remaining behavior. Although she couldn't make reintegration from Dad's house easier, she could be more understanding of how Josh might feel being shuffled back and forth.

Maria continued to track Josh's behavior for a few more weeks after starting Ignore it!.

Maria reported that she and Josh were having significantly fewer negative interactions and that when Josh did turn angry it never escalated because she used Ignore it!.

Figure 1: Josh's Cursing and Yelling

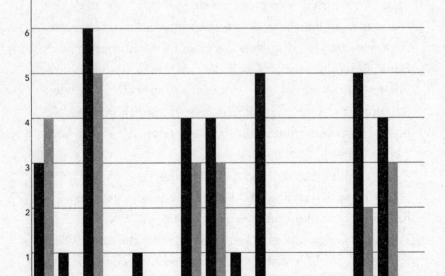

Conner's parents contacted me because their three-year-old son had excessive tantrums. They knew tantrums were common at this age, but it seemed Conner was really struggling to deal with even the slightest disturbances. Conner is the youngest of three boys. His brothers, ages nine and twelve, were both die-hard sports fanatics. They each played baseball and flag football all year. Conner liked to hang with the big boys and pretend he could do what they did. However, because of his age he obviously wasn't up to par. This was a constant source of frustration for the little guy. Conner's parents observed and tracked their youngest son's behavior for a week. Since he melted down often, we used a chart where they could just add a hash mark every time Conner lost it (I recommend this because it makes it easy to track and easy to see trends visually).

The results were illuminating (Figure 2, p. 204). The typical tantrum times for Conner were between noon and two in the afternoon, as well as the few hours before bedtime. He particularly struggled on the weekends (fourteen tantrums on Saturday and sixteen on Sunday).

After careful consideration, Conner's mom and dad could see why Saturdays and Sundays were a mess for Conner. His brothers each typically had two games a day. Since they were not on the same team, that meant the parents each had to take a boy individually to the game. Hence, Conner's weekends were spent being dragged from this field to that field and that field to this field. He didn't receive a quality nap or have any time when activities were structured around his needs. Meals tended to be late or on the go, and by the end of the day Conner was spent. To improve the situation even before using Ignore it! Conner's parents had their nine-year-old drop one sport. He didn't love football, so that was an easy choice. They also worked harder to coordinate rides for the older boys. While they would have loved to be at every game, they realized it wasn't fair (or healthy) for Conner to be considered lowest on the totem pole. When Mom and Dad really wanted to attend a game that might not work for Conner, they arranged for a babysitter. These small changes caused the frequency of weekend tantrums to plummet. Mom and Dad then focused on using Ignore it! during the week in the challenging times. Being alert to the difficult times helped them not miss the opportunity to use Ignore it!.

Figure 2: Conner's Tantrums

Toddler Tantrums	8–10 a.m.	10–12 p.m.	12–2 p.m.	2–4 p.m.	4–6 p.m.	6–8 p.m.
Monday		I	I			II
Tuesday						I
Wednesday			II			
Thursday			IIII			
Friday						IIII
Saturday		II	IIII	II	II	IIII
Sunday	I	II	IIII	III	III	II

Evaluation of Ignore It! and Rewards

Up until this point in the chapter, we have reviewed how to observe patterns in behavior prior to implementing Ignore it!. Baseline data helps parents work out some kinks in scheduling, meals, and even the parent-child relationship. But there is so much more tracking can tell us after beginning Ignore it!.

Allison was used to getting her way. Most of the time, her parents gave in to her post-tantrum demands. Still, it was impossible to allow Allison to fulfill every whim. When Allison got pushback from her parents, she would throw a Bigfoot-sized tantrum. Baseline tracking over five days showed that Allison typically had three to four tantrums daily. On day six, Allison's parents began to implement Ignore it! every time their daughter raged. They also started to use a reward chart, commending Allison for being respectful, for cleaning up after herself, and for sitting nicely at meals. These were all areas where Allison previously struggled and where tantrums often began.

Shortly after the launch of Ignore it! and the reward chart, Allison displayed an extinction burst (Figure 3, p. 206). She peaked with six tantrums on day nine. However, her parents kept at it with Ignore it! and the tantrums practically dropped off while the number of rewards simultaneously increased. Allison loved the reward chart. It allowed her to save points for a trip to the bookstore, her favorite place. By the end of the first week, she had practically earned enough stars for the Fancy Nancy book she had been eyeing.

Because Allison's parents simultaneously implemented Ignore it! and the reward chart, it is impossible to know for certain if the improved behavior is due to Ignore it!, the reward system, or both. For Allison's parents, however, it mattered not. Their daughter was happier, there were far fewer outbursts, and they were once again enjoying their time with their daughter.

Researchers often roll out interventions or remove them in stages to determine which intervention causes the change. But this method isn't recommended with Ignore it!. Previous research shows that Ignore it! and like interventions are much more effective when they are combined with positive reinforcement for appropriate behaviors. Allison's parents did just that and it worked like a charm.

Figure 3: Allison's Improvement with Reward Chart

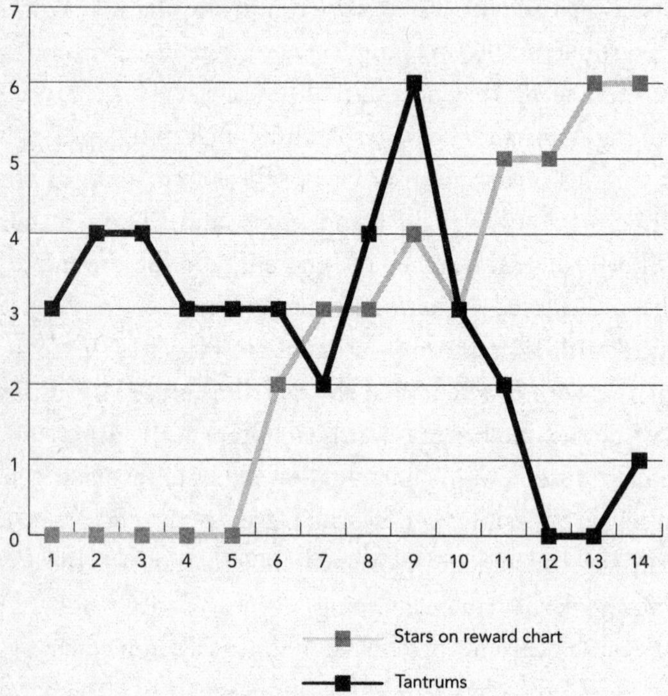

Stars on reward chart

Tantrums

Multiple Behaviors, One Chart

It is possible to track any number of undesirable behaviors at one time. However, I would recommend limiting tracking to two or three behaviors at one time. Tracking takes time and observation and can get a bit murky with too many behaviors to divert attention. You can always track another behavior at a later date. Sometimes parents work on a few issues at once. When those issues improve, they move on to other problematic behaviors. Below is a sample chart for tracking tantrums, yelling, and cursing. The parents who used this chart printed it out and carried it around all day in their pockets. They each tracked and compared the information.

Behavior	Monday	Tuesday	Wednesday	Thursday	Friday	Saturday	Sunday	Total
Tantrums								
Yelling								
Cursing								

Tracking Tips

- Don't discuss tracking with the child.
- Track no more than three behaviors at once. For most families, tracking two behaviors at a time is preferred.
- Do your tracking discreetly. Don't put the chart on the kitchen bulletin board. Keep it in a drawer or your pocket.
- If the behavior is very variable (meaning it appears inconsistently), you will need to track for longer. It is also possible that tracking might not be helpful because the behavior doesn't happen often enough to create a pattern.
- Tracking for three or four days to get the baseline is sufficient if the behavior happens frequently (several times every day).
- It is possible to skip the baseline phase. In fact, it isn't necessary at all. Some people decide just to keep track of behavior once beginning Ignore it!. This can be helpful to see improvement and see the extinction burst when it appears.

- If you find tracking annoying, frustrating, or too time-consuming, simply don't do it. Tracking should not take effort away from implementing Ignore it!. Chances are you will know when the behavior improves anecdotally, making the evaluation inconsequential.

CHAPTER 14

Frequently Asked Questions

For what age is Ignore it! most appropriate?

Ignore it! is recommended for children ages two to twenty-one. The program works on all ages once the child enters the toddler years. In fact, Ignore it! is perfect for irrational toddlers. The good news is that once you learn to Ignore it! you can use the technique until adulthood. Even kids who come home from college have unpleasant behaviors they may have picked up by being away from home. You can get the kids right back in shape with appropriate behavior by using Ignore it!.

How long does Ignore it! take to work?

It depends. I know that's probably not the answer you want, but it's true. One might see a slow and gradual change. Others may well experience an immediate, significant decrease in the targeted behavior. In general, the longer the behavior was rewarded, the longer it will take to eradicate. Similarly, the bigger the payoff/reward for the behavior, the harder it is to change. The last variable is behavior that has been intermittently rewarded. This means that sometimes you said no and meant it, but other times you gave in after a fuss. If behavior was only sometimes rewarded, it will also take longer to see the change. It's important to keep in mind that any progress is good progress. That's why I recommend using the tracking chart reviewed in Chapter 13. If you can see progress, it helps keep you going.

What if my child hits me or throws objects while I am ignoring?

It depends. If it is possible to Ignore it!, that's always the best option. Any reaction you give only serves as reinforcement for the act of hitting or throwing. Even if you turn angry, a child might still be motivated to behave similarly in the future. Withdrawing all attention sends the message that hitting and throwing will not accomplish the child's goals. However, if you are genuinely hurt by the aggression, put the child in an immediate time-out. Time-out is simply another way to practice Ignore it!, but in this case it helps break the battle of wills and removes the opportunity to continue hurting you. Unfortunately, putting a teen in time-out isn't really possible. So I revert to the original point—just continue to Ignore it!.

Would Ignore it! work in a classroom?

Yes! Ignore it! works beautifully in the classroom provided that other children in the classroom aren't reinforcing the undesirable behavior. If a child acts silly to gain attention and no one pays her any mind, the behavior will go away. But if the teacher is using Ignore it! while some of the children giggle or high-five the troublemaker, Ignore it! is not likely to improve the behavior. However, the teacher can work with the other children to reward their good behavior (as well as rewarding the class clown) so that over time everyone learns to ignore this difficult student.

Why am I still seeing some bad behavior?

There are several reasons you might still be seeing unwanted behavior after starting Ignore it!. Behavior could be still improving. Make sure to use the tracking chart so you can see if behavior is getting better. Sometimes it feels like there is no change, but there actually is. If it is improving—albeit slowly—keep plugging away. Another reason you may still see some remnants of the behavior is that they are age appropriate. For example, tantrums are typical behavior in children between the ages of two and four. However, with Ignore it!, these tantrums should become more infrequent and should also be significantly shorter, with less intensity. Last, it is possible that you are ignoring but also intermittently reinforcing. Sending mixed messages encourages children. Make sure to Ignore it! consistently each and every time you see the targeted behavior.

How should I discuss Ignore it! with my children before beginning?

This conversation is not necessary. Behavior speaks much louder than words. Furthermore, younger children will not fully understand the program until you actually commence.

And even then, their understanding will be tenuous. Luckily, it isn't necessary for children to comprehend or even be conscious of Ignore it! for it to be effective. I know for some of you it will feel impossible to Ignore it! without an explanation. So if you feel you absolutely cannot proceed without reviewing the program, then have a very brief powwow with your children. Simply tell them that you will be ignoring a few specific behaviors (tantrums, negotiating, whining, cursing, outburst), then let your actions do the talking. The message will be loud and clear when the rewards are removed from the child's behavior.

My daughter used to cry on command. She was dramatic and the tears were for effect and attention. Ignore it! has greatly improved her behavior, and we rarely see this kind of hysterics. However, how do I handle tears from a legitimate pain that are still blown out of proportion?

Always address real pain, disappointment, or hurt feelings. We don't want children to feel alone, shamed, or left without needed care. But for a child who is prone to histrionics, it is vital that you address the actual issue promptly and completely while ignoring the excessive reaction. If your daughter falls and cuts her knee, check on her. If she needs some sort of medical intervention (such as an ice pack or a Band-Aid), provide that. However, as soon as you have addressed the issue, begin Ignore it! to ward off providing reinforcement for the attention-seeking behavior. Remember to listen carefully and reengage quickly to redirect your daughter to another activity.

How much worse will behavior become during the extinction burst?

This is hard to predict. Behavior during the extinction burst can get worse in three different ways: increased intensity, increased frequency, and increased duration of each episode. Behavior can turn markedly worse and then quickly improve. Other times, it's possible behavior will take a bit longer to disappear. In general, the more consistent you are in ignoring all demonstrations of the targeted behavior, the more quickly the extinction burst will recede. From my personal experience, the extinction bursts typically don't last more than a few days. The ones that lasted the longest were due to children who had a long history of reinforcement for their behavior or whose parents were unable to Ignore it! consistently.

We messed up. We gave in to the extinction burst and the behavior is so much worse now. What should we do to get back on track?

Take a couple of deep breaths and use a day or two to regroup. It's okay—this sort of thing happens. Now reread Chapters 4, 5, and 12. Make sure you are clear on how to implement, then choose a day to begin again. Learn from your mistakes. Where did you go wrong? Was it really just giving in to the extinction burst or was there some inconsistency? Sometimes inconsistency can come from multiple caregivers sending different messages by handling the behavior differently. For example, if you are conscientiously administering Ignore it! but your babysitter offers Oreo cookies with the first hint of a whine, you will generally have a more difficult time. Make sure all caregivers, including those at day care and grandparents, are on board with the program. If needed, share this book so you can be sure they know what to do in each situation.

Isn't it bribery to use rewards to change behavior?

Nope. Bribery and rewards are not at all the same thing. Rewards sometimes get a bad rap. But life is full of naturally occurring rewards. I make dinner for a neighbor who has been ill. When the neighbor is feeling better, she thanks me for my kindness and tells me how much that dinner helped. I, in turn, feel a sense of happiness that I was able to help my neighbor. That warm, fuzzy, good feeling is a naturally occurring reward. As a professor, I am evaluated every year. If the scores on my evaluations are above a certain level, I receive a raise (aka: the reward). That raise is powerful incentive to continue to work hard the following year. That's the purpose of a reward—to motivate good behavior and hard work. Rewards are put into place to reinforce good behavior. An example of an appropriate reward for children would be, "If you keep your room clean for the entire week, you can go out for dinner on Friday."

Bribery involves using nefarious means to accomplish a goal. Bribes are most often offered to stop bad behavior. For example, "Stop crying and I'll let you watch your show." That's a bribe.

A reward would be given only if the crying never happened. If a child asked nicely to watch a show and didn't resort to holding the parent hostage, then a reward could be offered. So how can you be sure to offer rewards and not bribes? Well, rewards are never negotiated, and they are always given on your terms. Bribes are generally given after a child asks, "What will you give me if I [fill in the behavior]?" If you feel icky when giving the "prize" for the behavior, you probably succumbed to a bribe. However, if you provide a prize for good behavior that was set up prior to the exhibited behavior, it's a reward.

When I tell my daughter to do a required task, she shouts at me. She gets so aggressive that I stop wanting to talk to her. I walk away because I am afraid I will lose it on her. But then she gets out of doing the chore. How can I coerce her to stop shouting at me and to do the chore?

Your daughter is a smart cookie. She has figured out exactly how to get out of doing a task. If she turns nasty, you retreat. When you walk away, you are reinforcing her yelling and guaranteeing that the next time she doesn't feel like obliging with a chore she will begin shouting at you. It would be helpful for you to find ways to communicate with your daughter without losing your cool. Take deep breaths. Talk positively to yourself in your head. Practice what you want to say before heading into her room. Go to a happy place in your thoughts. Whatever you do, don't walk away. When she starts to rant at you, stand your ground and ignore all comments thrown your way. As soon as she takes a break, do not react to the tirade. Instead—in a calm voice—simply re-engage. If you continue to ask your daughter to do tasks and refuse to give her a reprieve from consequences due to avoidance tactics, this will pass. She will begin to accept the chores on the first try.

My four-year-old son knows that I can't deal with him banging his head on the wall when he is frustrated. So when I tell my son to clean up, he starts banging his head. How can I get him to stop?

If your son is a head banger, you might want to consult with a therapist trained in applied behavioral analysis (ABA) to help you implement Ignore it!. Check Appendix D for a referral website to help find a qualified therapist in your area. It is unclear from the question why your son might be banging his head. It may be for attention, to escape an annoying chore, or for some type of sensory input. All of these rewards for the behavior can be treated with Ignore it!. It is important to remove all benefits of the behavior. There are several ways to do that. Create a safe space for him so that it is nearly impossible to access a headbanging-friendly wall or hard surface. Alternatively, have him wear a helmet when he is playing with his toys. That way, when he bangs his head you will know he is less at risk for an injury and he may not get sensory satisfaction from doing it. Remember, as soon as the headbanging ceases, to immediately reengage. Also, don't forget to praise your son when he appropriately cleans up or transitions from one activity to another.

There are some behaviors that are still present after the extinction burst. My son continues to have some tantrums. How should I handle these?

For some children, it may be developmentally appropriate to have tantrums between the ages of two and four. But Ignore it! should drastically reduce the frequency, intensity, and duration. Continue to use Ignore it! on undesirable behaviors as needed. Over time, the behaviors will decrease further or may disappear altogether as the child develops more appropriate behaviors.

Our daughter plays with her hair constantly, and often pulls it out. We thought she did this for attention, so we started to Ignore it! But then we noticed that she also does it when she is alone in her room. How can we address the behavior if we aren't always present when it happens?

Your daughter may have other underlying issues that need to be addressed by a licensed counselor or doctor. I suggest holding off on Ignore it! until your daughter can have a full evaluation to understand why she is pulling hair. Ignore it! works in changing behavior only if the behavior is happening as a result of reinforcement. Thus, removing the reinforcement removes the reward. If your daughter is receiving another "reward" for the hair-pulling, then Ignore it! may not be effective. She could have trichotillomania (an impulse control disorder), anxiety, a medical condition, or another psychological issue. Ignore it! might still work very well with another treatment plan that incorporates treating the underlying cause for the behavior.

How quickly can we start to Ignore it!?

As soon as you have finished the book you can begin to use Ignore it!. You don't need to obtain any special equipment. You don't need to wait for any specific period of time. However, it is a good idea to begin Ignore it! when life isn't at its most stressful. So, if you are moving, bringing home a new baby, getting a divorce, school is beginning, or a close family member just passed away, maybe wait a bit for life to get back to normal. If your life never seems to settle down, then just get started.

When should I stop using Ignore it!?
Never! Ignore it! is a way of life. Being able to tune out annoyances or unwanted behavior is a skill that will serve you well through the years, and not only in parenting. The benefits of Ignore it! don't expire as the child ages and develops. That being said, it is important to remember that Ignore it! has designated phases (Ignore, Listen, Reengage, Repair), and once the last phase is reached, you move on. But at the next opportunity, begin Ignore It! again.

CHAPTER 15

The Pep Talk and Final Tips

We've had bad luck with our kids—they've all grown up.

—Christopher Morley

BEFORE I HAD children, I suppose I wasn't too different from most prospective parents. There were fantasies of what parenting and my children would be like. It all evoked images of extra-long Sunday snuggles and laughter. I imagined glorious road trips and family adventures. I pictured my kids eating wheat bread *with the crusts on* and enjoying every ethnic cuisine the world had to offer. Their hair would be neatly combed and their faces would be clean and glowing. Their clothes? Adorable. Their attitudes? Perfect. Their grades? Only As. My kids would behave at all times, use "please" and "thank you" without prompting, make friends with ease, have no hang-ups or anxieties. Oh, they would be afforded perfect health, too.

This might not surprise you, but my kids did not grow according to my warped fantasy. A great many of us, including myself, do not eat the crusts on bread. My kids are not geniuses. They aren't always polite and their table manners are incorrigible. They have plenty of hang-ups and problems (medical, social, and otherwise). They aren't grateful for everything that is ever given to them, and their attitudes sometimes, well, stink. As for their brushed hair, their clean faces, their precious outfits . . . sometimes, but, um, not that often. Not even close.

Not for nothing, I'm hardly the parent I pictured, either. I am significantly more tired than I imagined. That fatigue leads me to use shortcuts that weren't part of my plan. We have breakfast for dinner and/or supermarket rotisserie chicken at least once a week. We watch television probably more than recommended by the American Academy of Pediatrics. Worst of all, I'm definitely more annoyed and frustrated than my pre-parenthood apparition.

No one I know envisions real-life parenting before having children. Then, when the reality fails to match the dream, it is disorienting. Demoralizing. Sometimes even embarrassing. And because parents don't necessarily anticipate the struggles, they aren't particularly equipped to handle them. In a country where children (and parents) are often measured by the college sticker on the back of Mom and Dad's car, it is often impossible to meet the imaginary benchmarks we set for our children and ourselves.

As a society, we have elevated children and parenthood responsibilities to the level of national security. Ever infinitesimal decisions become gut-wrenching exercises. We micromanage and worry to the point of exhaustion, and ultimately parenting becomes a chore. But we rarely discuss the struggles out loud. We cry quietly at night. We feel guilt and shame, and we feel alone.

When our children were babies and toddlers, my husband

and I struggled with some of the responsibilities of parenting small children. We grappled to manage two careers and two very young kids. One day, while hosting some friends for dinner, I wondered if another mother felt as I did. I asked her, specifically, what percentage of the time parenting was a joy compared to the percentage when it was a chore or worse? Without a moment's pause she said, "I love being a mom 100 percent of the time. It's always a joy."

On the outside, I smiled. "Oh," I said, "that's wonderful."

On the inside, I was crushed. *Oh*, I thought, *I'm a terrible person*.

I love being a parent. My husband loves being a parent. But if I'm being completely honest, child rearing has never been a 100 percent joyful proposition for me. Sometimes it's 60 percent great. Sometimes it's 30. On the loveliest of days (sunny skies, painting pottery, ice cream), it's 80 percent. On the worst, it's more like 10 percent joy.

Parenting is work by definition. Sure, some of the work has become easier as my children have aged and turned more independent. But in other ways it is all the more difficult. Making lunches at six a.m., shuttling two kids to two different schools, early risers, stomach viruses, endless loads of laundry, errant LEGO pieces, doctor's appointments, and rushing from here to there at a breakneck pace are far from fun in my book. But they are the necessary tasks of parenthood. In other words, they are mostly unavoidable.

What *is* optional are the tantrums, the negotiating, the eye rolling, the nagging, the begging, and the yelling. The interminable delays at bedtime—avoidable. The begging for the latest and greatest iPhone—stoppable. The whining—needless.

Although it's work, being a mother or father should also be enjoyable. The highs should outweigh the lows. And they can. That's why I wrote this book, and why you're reading it. Our kids are kids for a fleeting period of time. They're born, we raise them, they're gone—*bam!*—in a blink. None of us wants to spend those years engaged in one everlasting struggle, one endless mental breakdown with arguments and whining and sloppy rooms.

So here's what you need to do: start. Yes, start. You've read the book. You have the information. Just get started. You don't need a big event to get started. You don't need to buy anything special to get started. And you don't need to wait for a vacation or time off to get started. Ignore it! doesn't take time away from doing anything else, because if you weren't ignoring the behavior, you would be addressing it. That certainly is more time-consuming. You only need to commit to it 100 percent.

What does 100 percent commitment look like? It's ignoring every time the opportunity arises. It's ignoring the behavior from start to finish. And it's not giving up when it's difficult or inconvenient. Commitment on the 100 percent level also means not aborting Ignore it! during the extinction burst. Remember, if it seems like the behavior is getting worse, Ignore it! is working. Hang in there, because after the burst is the extinction (the best part—where the behavior disappears).

Making a major change isn't a one-and-done situation. It's a process. A process refers to a series of steps taken to accomplish a goal. This is important to remember. There will be times when you forget to ignore. There will be times when you engage without thinking before the episode is over. There will be setbacks. But you just need to keep in mind that it's a process.

It may take you time to perfect Ignore it! . . . but I guarantee you can do it.

How can I be so certain? Because Ignore it! works. The research behind the method is tested and sound. If you aren't seeing the success you hoped for, reread the book. Take your time. Take new notes. Think about where you might have gone off track. Then begin again. Just don't give up. You can and should enjoy being a parent. Ignore it! can help.

I'm a family coach. I help people with parenting problems for a living. I use the same techniques I teach other families on my own children. And because of this, my kids are pretty good kids. They listen fairly well. They behave reasonably most of the time. And they generally keep annoying and inappropriate behaviors to a minimum. However, they are children, not robots. And for that matter, I'm not a robot, either. I falter. I make mistakes. And my daughter and son sometimes test the limits.

No one parents perfectly all the time. Not experts such as Dr. Sears and Dr. Ferber. Not former first ladies Laura Bush or Michelle Obama. Not even the fictional (and lovely) Carol Brady got it right all the time. On *The Brady Bunch*, Peter played basketball in the house (after being told not to) and broke a lamp. Alice sprained her ankle because the kids didn't put away their toys. Cindy was a constant tattler. Hey, this stuff even happens in idealistic sitcoms. So be kind to yourself. Forgive mistakes and transgressions. You are trying to make life better in your family for everyone. That's noble. Go you!

Over the course of writing this book, I kept a list of things I considered especially important—things I didn't want to forget to reinforce before sending you on your way toward parental bliss. . . .

- Relish small victories. A victory is a victory. Next time might be bigger.

- At any point, you can make a change. It's never too late to invest in a better relationship with your child. It's never a lost cause. Ever!

- Be flexible. There isn't always a right and a wrong way. Sometimes we get so focused on what we are sure is right, we forget that nothing terrible will happen if we consider another option.

- Don't ignore everything. Children need supervision, attention, and engagement. Ignore it! is only for annoying, inappropriate behaviors. Even if you think your child is annoying all day, you cannot ignore her 24/7. Pick a few behaviors to work on and try to balance ignoring with engaging.

- Talk to some friends and family about what you are doing so they don't intervene or think you are crazy.

- Keep a journal to track annoying behaviors, parenting satisfaction, and the relationship with your child. Sometimes changes are subtle or occur over time. If you are a person who enjoys writing or keeping a diary, I highly recommend this exercise. You will be amazed at how much can change.

- Say "please" and "thank you" to your children. Sometimes we forget to model the behaviors we would like to see. Getting in the habit of using polite requests and responses at every opportunity helps keep interactions positive and ensures praise for good behavior.

- Don't ask for what you want done. Tell your child specifically what you expect. Don't say, "Could you put the dishes

in the sink?" That sounds optional to me. Instead say, "Put
the dishes in the sink, please."

- Be patient. Change will come, but it may not be fast. Slow
progress is still progress.
- Pay close attention to any effort exhibited by children. Try
to read between the lines when relationships are strained.
If you request that laundry be put away and your child
does it but does it with a bad attitude, Ignore it!. If he puts
the laundry away but does a poor job of it, Ignore it!.
- Give yourself a break. You deserve it.

Here's the bottom line: You love your children, and that's
the most important thing. You want them to have happy lives,
to explore and engage and thrive. You want them to look back
upon these years with a glow. And you want to enjoy the
ride, too.

Sometimes this means wrapping your kids in a warm embrace and covering their faces with kisses.

Sometimes it means ignoring them.

Acknowledgments

The desire to write a book existed in me for years. For a variety of reasons, the time wasn't right. As friends, colleagues, and my husband published book after book, I struggled with why I hadn't done the same. However, this book could not have been written in this way ten years ago or five or even two. In my twenty-plus years working as a social worker and as The Family Coach, I have gained a tremendous amount of the theoretical knowledge, writing experience, and repetition with families that was needed to write this book. I didn't learn all of that in a vacuum. Along the way, there were many people who taught, helped, and supported me. Those people deserve to be recognized now because this book wouldn't be what it is without them.

Growing up, I wanted to help people as a career. But the only occupation that fit the bill was being a medical doctor. I went through high school and most of college planning to work with terminally ill children. I volunteered in hospitals year after year. But I always had a quiet voice in my head that said medicine wasn't for me. I couldn't deal with the gory parts of being a doctor. Then I heard that my mom's friend Ellen Nusblatt was going back to school to become a social worker. A what? I'd never heard of a social worker. Ellen exposed me to a world where one could help vulnerable people without the messy gore of the hospital. Social work turned out to be exactly what I wanted to do for the rest of my life. Ellen Nusblatt, thank you.

Every life choice, big or small, on purpose or by accident, changes the course of that life. In high school, when my parents divorced and I moved to New York City, I never imagined I would become friends with a girl named Ellie, and thirteen years later, I would meet my husband at that girl's wedding. My mother's decision (which I was fully against at the time) gave me the life I have now. That life includes the writer husband who has taught me everything I know about writing. I'd like to acknowledge that sometimes mothers do know best, so thank you, Mom. And a tremendous thank-you to Ellie, Jon, Allegra, and Ben Wertheim, who are so much more than friends. I am truly blessed with your support and encouragement. Ellie, I have no words for how much you mean to me. Thank you!

Elizabeth Evans got me off to a great start honing the proposal that would eventually land me a contract for this book. Coleen O'Shea is everything one could ask for in an agent. She's available, responsive, and I'd go to battle with her any day. Sara Carder at TarcherPerigee had tremendous enthusiasm for Ignore it! from day one. Thank you, Sara, for seeing my potential as an author and for helping make my baby into a book. I'd also like to thank Heather Brennan at TarcherPerigee for her hard work and for being an A+ problem solver.

Christopher John Farley at the *Wall Street Journal*, Pat Wiedenkeller at CNN, Amanda Sidman at the *Today* show, and B. J. Schecter at *Sports Illustrated* offered me big breaks and made me a better writer and speaker.

Before starting The Family Coach, I worked for years in the nonprofit world. Dave Gregorio, Elizabeth Foley, and all of my social work buddies from Covenant House provided me with an incredibly fulfilling learning experience. Those colleagues (too many to mention here, but you know who you are) continue to inspire me so many years later. Jill Murray Kuppinger and I have spent hundreds of hours running together processing clients, work, and life. I am forever indebted for her friendship and words of wisdom. Jill taught me that everything always works out in the end. If it hasn't worked out, then it isn't the end. Through Jill, I met Greg Kuppinger and Jeanne and Brant Beaupre. We started off as three social work friends, and now we have blossomed into three families, totaling twelve people. It's been a great ride. Mike and Sandi Friedman from Camp Vacamas were an inspiration and models in living a life devoted to a great cause.

If it's true that raising children takes a village, then the families on Taymil Road were my village. Through the years so many have helped and supported my work and my family. The Waxlers, Goonetilekes, Lees, Epperson-Farleys, Moscowitz-Urbases, Cohens, Dalloses, and Edelsons, and Chuck Drago, Terry Gattan, and Elaine Klein made our street feel like living in Mayberry. A special shout-out to Diane, Larry, Phoebe, and James Luftig for all the meals, long snow days by the fire, and doggie playdates. Laurel Turnbull watched my babies for a few years while I went back to school. She loved my kids like her own so I could focus on my studies.

There are friends who have been so much more than friends. Their support for me knew no bounds. Rachel Zients and Amy Bass talked writing and books and made me feel like I could do this book. Noel Besuzzi, photographer extraordinaire, is one of the most encouraging and giving people I have ever met. I'm so grateful for her friendship and every one of her insights. Colleagues Mike and Margaret Moodian and Sheila Steinberg from Brandman University were terrific mentors and friends. Michael Lewis lent his critical editorial eye to *Ignore It!*, and his enthusiasm provided much-needed encouragement.

There are so many other people who in ways big and small have supported me and my work. I'd like to thank the following people, who are listed in no particular order: Chris Berman, David Pearlman, the Parnaby family, Jen Monti, Paul Olkowski, Samara Harris, Mali Workman, Michelle Nicoloff, the Webb family, Carmen Hendricks, Jade Docherty, the Gregerman family, the Corbo family, the Blaisdell family, the Chasman family, Dina Bortnichak, Mookie Luftig, Norma Rose Pearlman, Rebecca Lerner, Lata Murti, Dan Jahns, Alex Silverman, Michael Dunne, Sara Russell, Michelle Maidenberg, Dara Kurtz, Alison Cimmet, Desa Philadelphia, Alison Zarchan, Jennifer Brinkman, Jennifer Katz, Dana Resnik, Shefali Tsabary, Dave Coverly, Michele Bock, Kristen Riolo, everyone at Stroller Strides, and last but definitely not least, Luba Bigun.

I've been blessed with the opportunity to teach nontraditional college students for the past eight years. The students and faculty at Yeshiva University, College of New Rochelle, and Brandman University have kept me on my game. These students have taught me everything one needs to know about dedication and resiliency.

I started The Family Coach because I wanted to help parents resolve everyday problems so they could enjoy parenting more. Over the years, I have met many incredible families. They asked me to come into their homes and allowed me to observe them when they felt most uneasy and exposed. Their issues are universal and provided the detail and scenarios in this book. I owe all of these families a great deal of gratitude for their trust and hard work.

I have the two best sisters. Leah Guggenheimer has been a role model and cheerleader for me all my life. She knows how to handle my hysterical late-night phone calls better than anyone else. I waited seventeen years for a little sister, and when Jessica Guggenheimer finally arrived, she was worth the wait. Jordan and Isaiah Williams provide me with the joy of being an aunt, which is so different from being a parent.

My parents, Richard Guggenheimer and Laura Cole, somehow gave me the confidence that I could do anything I set out to do. Over the years, I've been able to accomplish more than I ever dreamed because of their uninterrupted support. Rodney Cole has provided chocolate whenever I've needed it most for the past thirty years. Joan and Stanley Pearlman are truly the best in-laws in the land. They gush over my successes just as they would for their own son's (often more). My grandmother Norma Shapiro is an inspiration to many. Her fortitude, dedication, hard work, and total devotion to her family are gifts I hope I can repay to my own grandkids.

Emmett and Casey Pearlman are the proof in my pudding. These kids keep me going and doing if only to show them that someday they can, too. I love you both to the moon and back.

I am so lucky Jeff Pearlman asked to marry me. Every accomplishment I have is due in large part to his support. He cooks, cleans, does laundry, puts the kids to bed, packs lunches, meets with the PTA, makes playdates, and so much more. Anything I can do as a mother, he can do, too. Thank you for this life we have made. Still, I could not ask for more.

Glossary of Terms

Antecedent: The action that cues or prompts the learned behavior to occur.

Applied behavioral analysis: The method of applying interventions scientifically to improve behavior to a meaningful degree.

Assessment: Systematic measurement of an intervention.

Baseline: Assessment of behavior before an intervention.

Behavior: The way a child acts.

Behavior modification: The systematic application of principles and techniques to assess and improve behavior.

Consequence: Anything that comes after a certain behavior; a result or effect of an action or condition. Consequences can be in the form of rewards or punishments.

External reinforcement: Someone or something provides outside motivation for behavior in the form of tangible rewards or verbal acknowledgment.

Extinction: The process of eliminating or reducing a conditioned response by not enforcing it.

Extinction burst: A temporary increase in frequency, duration, or intensity of behavior during the extinction process of Ignore it!.

Intermittent reinforcement: Behavior is reinforced irregularly.

Internal reinforcement: The benefit or motivation for behavior comes from within the child.

Logical consequence: A response to behavior that is set forth by the parent as a learning tool for children to remember discomfort and avoid behavior in the future.

Natural consequence: An outcome to an action that is unplanned by the parent and occurs naturally.

Negative reinforcement: Behavior is encouraged by simply taking away something undesirable.

Operant conditioning: A type of learning in which behavior is modified by consequences.

Positive reinforcement: Encouraging behavior by offering something desirable in response to the behavior.

Positive reinforcer: An item or action that increases the likelihood of a behavior when it is presented immediately following the behavior.

Reinforcement: Any process that encourages learning of a behavior. The behavior can be desirable or undesirable.

Reward: A pleasurable item or experience given in response to a behavior.

Token economy: A behavior modification program that awards children with theoretical or real tokens that can be exchanged for an alternate reward at a later time.

Unintentional extinction: Inadvertently removing attention and benefits from behavior that was desirable.

Age-Appropriate Rewards

P: Appropriate for Preschoolers

E: Appropriate for Children in Elementary School

M: Appropriate for Children in Middle School (Junior High)

HS: Appropriate for Children in High School

P	E	M	HS	Reward
		x	x	Music lessons
x	x	x		Visit the pet store or animal shelter to visit with the animals
x	x	x	x	A sweet treat
x	x	x	x	Visit a museum
x	x	x	x	Bake a treat
x	x	x	x	Watch a movie
x	x	x		Treat in lunch box for school
x	x	x	x	Candy
x	x	x		Television show

P	E	M	HS	Reward
x	x			Make a craft
x	x			Surprise with a decorated bedroom
x	x			Visit a favorite relative or friend
x	x			An extra book or story at bedtime
x	x			Create a fun surprise scavenger hunt around the house or yard
x	x			Collect flowers and leaves from the garden and make a bouquet or press in a book
x	x			Art project
x	x			Trip to the library
x	x			Make a giant fort with every pillow and sheet in the house
x	x			Trip to the zoo
x	x			Glow stick or lighting sparklers
x	x			Picnic
x	x			Make a garden
x	x			Treasure chest
x	x			Erasers
x				Paint pet rocks
x				Visit to the local fire department
x				Trip to the park
x				Coin-operated ride
x				Piggyback ride
x				Finger painting
x				Stickers
	x	x	x	Have favorite meal prepared for dinner
	x	x	x	Camp out in the backyard
	x	x	x	Choice of after-dinner activity
	x	x	x	Choice of game for game night
	x	x	x	Have a later bedtime (5–30 minutes)
	x	x	x	Haircut, braids, or hair dye
	x	x	x	Make a movie or video starring your child

P	E	M	HS	Reward
	x	x	x	Karaoke
	x	x	x	Alone time with one parent
	x	x	x	Extra time for video game, computer, television
	x	x	x	Get a ride to school instead of riding the bus
	x	x	x	Art or school supplies
	x	x	x	Paint child's room
	x	x	x	Book or audiobook from the bookstore
	x	x	x	Sign child up for a special class: singing, acting, karate, art, etc.
	x	x	x	Go fishing
	x	x	x	Rent a boat
	x	x	x	Have a date night with your child
	x	x	x	Go out for a meal
	x	x	x	Rent/buy a new movie
	x	x	x	Popcorn at the movies
	x	x	x	Control of music or radio station for the car
	x	x	x	Bowling, ice skating, roller skating, swimming
	x	x	x	Time off from chores
	x	x	x	Poster for bedroom
	x	x	x	Magazine subscription
	x	x	x	Trip to amusement park
	x	x	x	Invite a friend on a family trip or out for a meal
	x	x	x	Accessories: sports, hair, attire
	x	x	x	Download music
	x	x	x	Time with parent to do anything child wants (within reason)
	x	x	x	Time online
x				Bubble bath
		x	x	Cooking privilege
		x	x	Redecorate child's room
		x	x	Get to sit in the front seat of the car
		x	x	Lend the child a piece of your clothes, shoes, or jewelry

P	E	M	HS	Reward
		x	x	Money for shopping
		x	x	Trip to mall
		x	x	Concert
		x	x	Slumber party
		x	x	Chance to earn extra money
		x	x	Opt out of family activity
		x	x	Gift certificate
		x	x	Cell phone or upgrade
		x	x	Allowed to sleep in extra late on weekend
			x	Opportunity to borrow the car
			x	Give your child a piece of your jewelry

APPENDIX C

Sample Charts

*All Charts available for download at
www.TheFamilyCoach.com.

A-B-C Chart

Scenario with Time and Location	Antecedent	Behavior	Consequence	What Is Learned?

Parent Feeling Behavior Trigger Rating Chart

Day	Time	Parent Feeling Rating Scale 1–10 1: Happy as a clam 10: Intensely frustrated, angry, or at breaking point	Precipitating Incident	Parent Reaction	Identify Trigger

239

Nonreader Behavior Tracking Chart for Rewards

Pictures of Behavior	Monday	Tuesday	Wednesday	Thursday	Friday	Saturday	Sunday
TOTALS							

Picture	Reward	Point Value
	M&M's (1 for each point)	1
	5 mintues later bedtime	5
	A trip out for ice cream	20
	$10 to spend at a toy store	50

Behavior Tracking Chart for Older Child

Behavior	Monday	Tuesday	Wednesday	Thursday	Friday	Saturday	Sunday
TOTALS							

If I get 5 points, then I can have 5 extra minutes to play before bedtime.

If I get 10 points, then I can have a small sweet treat (cereal, marshmallow, chocolate chips).

If I get 20 points, then I can take a trip to the ice-cream store.

If I get 35 points, then I can have a turn in the kitchen making something.

If I get 50 points, then I can have a toy or a book from Barnes & Noble.

Behavior Tracking Chart for Evaluation

Behavior	Monday	Tuesday	Wednesday	Thursday	Friday	Saturday	Sunday	Total

APPENDIX D

Recommended Resources

Bronson, Po, and Ashley Merryman. *Nurture Shock*. New York: Twelve, 2009.

This research-driven and thoughtfully written book about how as parents we sometimes shouldn't trust our instincts fascinated me. The authors address a diverse range of topics such as praise, sibling relationships, intelligence and being gifted, self-control, and teen rebellion. This book will change the way you understand child development.

Dornfest, Asha. *Parent Hacks: 134 Genius Shortcuts for Life with Kids*. New York: Workman Publishing Company, 2016.

Parent Hacks provides essential out-of-the-box thinking, offering 134 creative solutions to the most common parenting annoyances. Covering mealtime, bath, sleep, getting dressed, potty, and travel, even the most seasoned parent can learn a clever workaround for a troublesome parenting woe.

Faber, Adele, and Elaine Mazlish. *Siblings without Rivalry: Help Your Children Live Together So You Can Live, Too*. New York: W. W. Norton & Company, 2012.

This is required reading for anyone who is thinking about having or who has at least two children. Written with a light and interesting style, this book demystifies sibling relationships and exposes the hidden mistakes parents often make that fuel rivalries.

Fraker, Cheryl, Mark Fishbein, Sibyl Cox, and Laura Walbert. *Food Chaining: The Proven 6-Step Plan to Stop Picky Eating, Solve Feeding Problems, and Expand Your Child's Diet.* New York: Marlowe & Company, 2007.

By far, this is the best book I have found to help parents comprehend a vast variety of food and feeding issues. The authors explain all of the issues and provide understandable concrete steps to improve eating. I have used this program with my child and with many in my practice. It's terrific.

Lahey, Jessica. *The Gift of Failure: How the Best Parents Learn to Let Go So Their Children Can Succeed.* New York: HarperCollins Publishers, 2015.

Allowing kids to make mistakes and sometimes fail is essential to future success. The author works through various areas of parenting, showing parents how to step back and let natural consequences and internal motivation kick in.

Lythcott-Haims, Julie. *How to Raise an Adult: Break Free of the Overparenting Trap and Prepare Your Kid for Success.* New York: Henry Holt & Company, 2016.

The premise is that overparenting is based on a fear that our children will not be successful as adults if we don't stay involved in every detail of their upbringing. The author, as the former freshman dean at Stanford, saw the effects of overinvolvement reach an apex. She offers well-balanced advice for how to step back and raise adults in a helicoptering epidemic.

Phelan, Thomas. *1-2-3 Magic: Effective Discipline for Children 2–12*. Naperville, IL: Sourcebooks, Inc., 2016.

Dr. Phelan offers a simple yet effective technique to inspire children to do their chores, listen to requests, and be more cooperative by using consequences.

Skinner, B. F. *Walden Two*. Indianapolis, IN: Hackett Publishing Company, Inc., 2005.

Classic fictional utopia dreamed up by B. F. Skinner, the founder of behaviorism. While this book was written in 1948 and has received reviews running the gamut, it is still worth a glance if you are interested in Skinner's inner beliefs.

Tsabary, Dr. Shefali. *Out of Control: Why Disciplining Your Child Doesn't Work . . . and What Will*. Vancouver, Canada: Namaste Publishing, 2013.

Dr. Tsabary holds up a mirror from which to view our parenting. Carefully constructed with plenty of anecdotes, *Out of Control* helps parents understand how they control their child, how an unresolved past interferes with their relationship with their children, and how punishments undercut children's abilities to learn self-discipline. This is a different kind of parenting read but worth digging into to broaden and deepen the basic principles of parenting.

WEBSITES

American Academy of Child & Adolescent Psychiatry, http://www.aacap.org/

American Psychological Association, www.apa.org

Autism Speaks, www.autismspeaks.org/

Behavior Analyst Certification Board, http://bacb.com/

The Incredible Years, http://incredibleyears.com/

Notes

Epigraph

xi   **"If there is anything that we wish to change in the . . ."**
Carl Jung, *Integration of the Personality* (New York: Farrar &
Rinehart, 1939), 285.

Chapter 1

21   **In a nationally representative study, 90 percent of American
parents admitted to harsh verbal discipline. This is equally
true both for parents of toddlers and those with a teenager living at home.**
Murray A. Straus and Carolyn J. Field, "Psychological aggression
by American parents: National data on prevalence, chronicity,
and severity," *Journal of Marriage and Family* 65, no. 4 (November
2003): 795–808.

21   **Not only does repetitive verbal discipline increase depression
in children, it also increases conduct problems.**
Ming-Te Wang and Sarah Kenny, "Longitudinal links between
fathers' and mothers' harsh verbal discipline and adolescents'
conduct problems and depressive symptoms," *Child Development*
85, no. 3 (May 2014): 908–923.

Chapter 2

24 **"A person who has been punished is not thereby simply less inclined to behave in a given way; at best, he learns how to avoid punishment."**
B. F. Skinner, *Beyond Freedom and Dignity* (New York: Knopf, 1971), 81.

35 **The concept of extinction is defined as the process of eliminating or reducing a conditioned response by not reinforcing it.**
"Extinction," Merriam-Webster.com, accessed May 8, 2016, http://www.merriam-webster.com/dictionary/extinction.

39 **The concept of extinction and behavior modification was used in an interesting study about bullying.**
Scott W. Ross, Robert H. Horner, and Thomas Higbee, "Bully prevention in positive behavior support," *Journal of Applied Behavior Analysis* 42, no. 4 (December 2009): 747–759.

Chapter 3

47 **Thus, behavior that is reinforced intermittently is more resistant to change.**
Gary Martin and Joseph Pear, *Behavior Modification: What It Is and How to Do It* (Upper Saddle River, N.J.: Prentice Hall, 1999).

Chapter 6

91 **It has been found to be highly successful in reducing talking back, noncooperation, oppositionality, destruction of property, yelling, nagging, hitting, and biting. It's also effective with children who have been diagnosed with a variety of developmental disorders.**
Gregory Fabiano, William Pelham Jr., Michael J. Manos, et al., "An evaluation of three time-out procedures for children with attention-deficit/hyperactivity disorder," *Behavior Therapy* 35, no. 3 (Summer 2004): 449–469.
Ronald Drabman and Greg Jarvie, "Counseling parents of children with behavior problems: The use of extinction and time-out techniques," *Pediatrics* 59, no. 1 (January 1977): 78–85.
Amy Drayton, "Deconstructing the time-out: What do mothers understand about a common disciplinary procedure?," accessed

August 31, 2016, http://commons.emich.edu/cgi/viewcontent .cgi?article=1909&context=theses.

91   **The Internet offers loads of faulty or inaccurate information about time-out.**
Amy Drayton, Melissa Anderson, Rachel Knight, Barbara Felt, Emily Fredericks, and Dawn Dore-Stites. "Internet guidance on time-out: Inaccuracies, omissions, and what to tell parents instead," *Journal of Developmental and Behavioral Pediatrics* 35, no. 4 (May 2014): 239–246.

95   **However, some evidence shows that time-outs lasting one to two minutes might be too easy an out.**
Ibid.

98   **If you see inappropriate behavior, give no more than one warning that if the behavior continues there will be a time-out.**
Mark Roberts, "The effects of warned versus unwarned time-out procedures on child noncompliance," *Child & Family Behavior Therapy* 4, no. 1 (January 1983): 37–53.
Janet Twyman, Happy Johnson, Jennifer Buie, and C. Michael Nelson, "The use of a warning procedure to signal a more intrusive time-out contingency," *Behavioral Disorders* 19, no. 4 (August 1994): 243–253.

102   **Follow through with time-out once it is initiated. Don't allow any arguing or fleeing to obviate the time-out.**
David Reitman and Ronald S. Drabman, "Read my fingertips: A procedure for enhancing the effectiveness of time-out with argumentative children," *Child & Family Behavior Therapy* 18, no. 2 (June 1996): 35–40.

Chapter 7

105   **JetBlue acknowledged how tough flying . . .**
"JetBlue aims to change stigma of crying babies in powerful new ad," Today.com, accessed June 20, 2016, http://www.today.com /parents/jetblue-aims-change-stigma-crying-babies-powerful -new-ad-t90316.

107   **Consider what happened to Matt and Melissa Graves of Elkhorn, Nebraska.**
"Sheriff: Body of toddler found after Florida alligator attack," *USA Today*, accessed July 1, 2016, http://www.usatoday.com

/story/news/2016/06/14/reports-alligator-drags-child-into -water-fla/85905266/.

107   **"An alligator being an alligator. Parent's [*sic*] not being parents."** Accessed August 30, 2016, https://twitter.com/domcena/status /743142682139070464.

107   **"Oh great, more innocent animals being killed because of piss poor parenting. Stop the world. I want to get off."** Accessed August 30, 2016, https://twitter.com/englane/status /74307536 7569739776.

107   **"I'm not sad about a 2yo being eaten by a gator bc his daddy ignored signs."** "Feminist says she doesn't care about alligator killing toddler: 'So finished with white men's entitlement,'" *The Daily Wire*, accessed August 30, 2016, http://www.dailywire.com /news/6701/feminist-says-she-doesnt-care-about-alligator -amanda-prestigiacomo.

108   **Country singer Jana Kramer found this out the hard way . . .** "Country star fires back at mom shamers with viral instagram post," *The Huffington Post*, accessed July 20, 2016, http:// www.huffingtonpost.com/entry/country-star-fires -back-at-mom-shamers-with-viral-instagram-post_us _5760109be4b071ec19ef2ac4.

109   **His theory of the transitional object is why all kids today have a lovey.** Donald W. Winnicott, "Transitional Objects and Transitional Phenomena: A Study of the first not-me possession," *The International Journal of Psychoanalysis* 32, no. 2 (January 1953): 89–97.

109   **Winnicott is also known for his concept of the "good enough mother."** Savithiri Ratnapalan and Helen Batty, "To be good enough," *Canadian Family Physician* 55, no. 3 (March 2009): 239–240, accessed August 30, 2016, http://www.ncbi.nlm.nih.gov/pmc /articles/PMC2654842/#b1-0550239.

Chapter 8

119   **When using Ignore it!, behavior can sometimes get worse for a short period before it improves. This is known as an extinction burst. It is actually a well-researched phenomenon.**

Alan E. Kazdin, *Behavior Modification in Applied Settings*, 7th ed. (Pacific Grove, CA: Brooks/Cole, 1994).

119 **Studies show that the targeted behavior you are ignoring can increase in magnitude, frequency, and duration before improving.**
Dorothea C. Lerman, Brian A. Iwata, and Michele D. Wallace, "Side effects of extinction: Prevalence of bursting and aggression during the treatment of self-injurious behavior," *Journal of Applied Behavior Analysis* 32, no. 1 (March 1999): 1–8, accessed August 31, 2016, http://www.ncbi.nlm.nih.gov/pmc/articles/PMC1284537/pdf/10201100.pdf.

Chapter 9

133 **"The ideal of behaviorism is to eliminate coercion: to apply controls by changing the environment in such a way as to reinforce the kind of behavior that benefits everyone."**
Dava Sobel, "B. F. Skinner, the champion of behaviorism, is dead at 86," *The New York Times*, 1990, accessed August 31, 2016, http://www.nytimes.com/1990/08/20/obituaries/b-f-skinner-the-champion-of-behaviorism-is-dead-at-86.html?pagewanted=all.

134 **Studies show that extinction (Ignore it!) is much more successful in eliminating undesirable behaviors when combined with positive reinforcement. Furthermore, the potential for an extinction burst (you know, the behavior getting worse before it gets better) is also diminished when reinforcement is applied to appropriate behaviors.**
Alan E. Kazdin, *Behavior Modification in Applied Settings*, 7th ed. (Pacific Grove, CA: Brooks/Cole, 1994).
Dorothea C. Lerman and Brian Iwata, "Developing a technology for the use of operant extinction in clinical settings: An examination of basic and applied research," *Journal of Applied Behavior Analysis* 29, no. 3 (Fall 1996): 345–382.
Dorothea C. Lerman, Brian A. Iwata, Bridget A. Shore, BA, and Sung Woo Kahng, "Responding maintained by intermittent reinforcement: Implications for the use of extinction with problem behavior in clinical settings," *Journal of Applied Behavior Analysis* 29, no. 2 (June 1996): 153–171.

135   **When parents recognize the rewards children are obtaining through nefarious means and apply those same rewards to appropriate behaviors, the parenting game is forever changed. Inappropriate behavior decreases while desirable behavior increases.**
Alan E. Kazdin, *Behavior Modification in Applied Settings,* 7th ed. (Pacific Grove, CA: Brooks/Cole, 1994).
Alan E. Kazdin, PhD, *The Kazdin Method for Parenting the Defiant Child* (New York: Houghton Mifflin Company, 2008).

137   **This fear is only partially supported by research.**
Christopher P. Cerasoli, Jessica M. Nicklin, and Michael T. Ford, "Intrinsic motivation and extrinsic incentives jointly predict performance: A 40-year meta-analysis," *Psychological Bulletin* 140, no. 4 (February 2014): 980.
Gary Martin and Joseph Pear, *Behavior Modification: What It Is and How to Do It,* 10th ed. (New York: Routledge, 2016).

Chapter 10

152   **"The consequences of an act affect the probability of its occurring again."**
Ty Patton, "Common sense and the common law, they're not as common as they used to be: A critique of the Kansas Supreme Court's new application of the collateral source rule," accessed August 31, 2016, http://heinonline.org/HOL/LandingPage ?handle=hein.journals/wasbur50&div=27&id=&page=.

153   **Furthermore, the testing is performed at such a high level that drug use can be detected up to six months back.**
Bill Gifford, "The *Scientific American* guide to cheating in the Olympics," *Scientific American,* 2016, accessed August 31, 2016, http://www.scientificamerican.com/article/the-scientific -american-guide-to-cheating-in-the-olympics/.

159   **In an effort to curb parental interruption of a teachable moment involving natural consequences, the Catholic High School for Boys . . .**
"Parents who bring forgotten lunch to school see shocking orders posted on door," *Conservative Tribune,* accessed August 31, 2016, http://conservativetribune.com/parents-see-shocking-orders/.

164   **There are four characteristics of consequences that allow the parents to help the child learn what behavior is undesirable.**

Jane Nelson, "The three R's of logical consequences, the three R's of punishment, and the six steps for winning children over." *Individual Psychology: Journal of Adlerian Theory, Research & Practice* 41, no. 2 (1985).

Chapter 11

171   **"An ounce of prevention is worth a pound of cure."**
Daniel Kiel, "An ounce of prevention is worth a pound of cure: Reframing the debate about law school affirmative action," *Denver University Law Review* 88, no. 4 (2010): 791–806, accessed August 31, 2016, http://www.law.du.edu/Documents/Denver-University-Law-Review/V88-4/Kiel_Toprinter_92611.pdf.

174   **Studies show that snacking has increased dramatically over the last forty years. Now snacking accounts for 27 percent of children's daily calorie count.**
Carmen Piernas and Barry M. Popkin, "Trends in snacking among U.S. children," *Health Affairs* 29, no. 3 (March 2010): 398–404, accessed August 31, 2016, http://content.healthaffairs.org/content/29/3/398.full?sid.

180   **Studies show that in the aftermath of exercise, thinking skills, self-control, memory, and school performance all improve. And these effects have been shown to be equally true for kids with attention deficit disorder (ADD) or without any diagnosis.**
Yu-Kai Chang, Suyen Liu, Hui-Hsiang Yu, and Yuan-Hung Lee, "Effect of acute exercise on executive function in children with attention deficit hyperactivity disorder," *Archives of Clinical Neuropsychology* 27, no. 2 (March 2012): 225–237.
Matthew Pontifex, Brian J. Saliba, Lauren B. Raine, Daniel L. Picchietti, and Charles H. Hillman. "Exercise improves behavioral, neurocognitive, and scholastic performance in children with attention deficit/hyperactivity disorder," *The Journal of Pediatrics* 162, no. 3 (March 2013): 543–551.
Gwen Dewar, "Exercise for children: Why keeping kids physically fit is good for the brain and helpful in the classroom," *Parenting Science*, accessed August 31, 2016, http://www.parentingscience.com/exercise-for-children.html.

180   **So how much exercise do children need to reap those benefits? In many cases, as little as twenty minutes.**

Matthew Pontifex, Brian J. Saliba, Lauren B. Raine, Daniel L. Picchietti, and Charles H. Hillman, "Exercise improves behavioral, neurocognitive, and scholastic performance in children with attention deficit/hyperac tivity disorder," *The Journal of Pediatrics* 162, no. 3 (March 2013): 543–551.

181 **For example, one study showed that children whose parents praised them at an early age for their good manners grew to have better social skills.**
"The effects of praise: What scientific studies reveal about the right way to praise kids," *Parenting Science*, accessed August 31, 2016, http://www.parentingscience.com/effects-of-praise.html.

Chapter 15

219 **"We've had bad luck with our kids—they've all grown up."**
BrainyQuote, accessed August 24, 2016, http://www.brainyquote.com/quotes/quotes/c/christophe104525.html?src=t_parenting.

235 **"100 Free Rewards for Parents to Give Their Children,"**
Behavior Doctor Seminars, accessed January 13, 2017, http://behaviordoctor.org/for-parents/. Kazdin, PhD, *The Kazdin Method for Parenting the Defiant Child*, 265.

About the Author

Dr. Catherine Pearlman is the founder of The Family Coach, a private practice that makes home visits to help parents with typical parenting issues. Her mission is to help parents enjoy their parenting and kids more. To that end, she advises on all matters of parenting such as potty and sleep training, discipline, food issues, sibling rivalry, and more. She has been a featured speaker for PTA gatherings, parent meetings, Moms Night Out, the *Wall Street Journal* Parenting Panel, nonprofit groups, and academic conferences around the country. She also conducts parenting seminars relating to practical parenting, behavior modification, setting expectations, and much more.

In addition to her private practice, Dr. Pearlman is also an assistant professor in the social work program at Brandman University. She writes the nationally syndicated "Dear Family Coach" column. Her articles on various topical issues have appeared in the *Wall Street Journal*, CNN.com, *Sports Illustrated*, and the *Huffington Post*, and she has been featured several times on NBC's *Today* show. Dr. Pearlman has also contributed to articles in *Parenting, National Geographic, Men's Health, Westchester Magazine*, the *Globe and Mail*, the *Journal News*, the *Orange County Register, Western New York Family Magazine, Parent Herald*, and *American Baby*. Internationally recognized as a parenting expert, Dr. Pearlman's columns have also appeared online in Australia, England, Canada, Kenya, and South Africa.

Dr. Pearlman received her doctorate in social welfare at Yeshiva University and her master's degree in social work from New York University. Her bachelor's degree in the history of medicine and sociology is from Bucknell University. She lives in California with her husband, two (mostly) well-behaved children, and dog, Norma.

Stay in Touch:

- Request for Dr. Pearlman to speak at your school or parent group by e-mailing her at Catherine@TheFamilyCoach.com.
- Connect with Dr. Pearlman on Facebook @TheFamilyCoach
- Follow Dr. Pearlman on Twitter @TheFamilyCoach.
- Learn more about Dr. Pearlman and her work as The Family Coach at www.TheFamilyCoach.com.

Also from TarcherPerigee

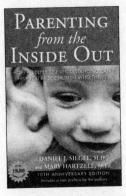

"Dan Siegel and Mary Hartzell have quite deftly managed to translate highly complex neuroscientific and psychological matters into lay strategies for effective parenting."

—Marilyn B. Benoit, MD, former president, American Academy of Child & Adolescent Psychiatry
978-1-10166-269-4 $17.00

"If there's one thing parents need to teach their kids—well beyond getting into college or finding a job—it's how to be humble, contributing citizens of the world. If you're a weary parent trying to do just that, you'll find encouragement and practical know-how in the clear and enjoyable pages of this book."

—Daniel H. Pink,
New York Times bestselling author of *Drive: The Surprising Truth About What Motivates Us*
978-0-39916-997-7 $16.00

"A must read! *If I Have to Tell You One More Time* delivers practical, step-by-step tools for well-behaved kids and happy families."

—Dr. Michele Borba, author of
The Big Book of Parenting Solutions and *Today* show contributor
978-0-39916-059-2 $15.95